MW00651235

Grow Your Medical Practice and Get Your Life Back

David Finkel
Pariksith Singh, MD
Alan Gassman, JD, LL.M

Copyright © 2018 David Finkel, Pariksith Singh, Alan Gassman. All rights reserved.

Published by Bradstreet and Sons, a division of New Edge Financial, LLC.

Creating Books that Build Businesses™

All rights reserved. No part of the material protected by this copyright may be reproduced or utilized in any form, electronic or mechanical, including photocopying, recording, scanning, or by any information storage and retrieval system, except as permitted under Section 107 or 108 of the 1976 United States Copyright Act, without written permission from the copyright owner.

This publication is designed to provide accurate and authoritative information in regard to the subject matter covered. It is sold with the understanding that the publisher is not engaged in rendering legal, accounting, or other professional service. If legal advice or other expert assistance is required, the service of a competent professional person should be sought.

While the publisher and author have used their best efforts in preparing this book, they make no representations with respect to the accuracy or completeness of the contents of this book and specifically disclaim any implied warranties of merchantability or fitness for a particular purpose. Neither the publisher nor author shall be liable for any loss of profit or any other commercial damages, including but not limited to special, incidental, consequential, or other damages.

Maui Mastermind® and Level Three Map™ are exclusive trademarks of Maui Mastermind (NV), LLC and are used with permission.

ISBN 978-0-692-06393-4

Printed in the United States of America

10 9 8 7 6 5 4 3 2 1

CONTENTS

FOREWORD

I n the summer of 1984 I took a trip across a sultry India with my mother and brother. Perhaps to help us pass the time, my mother told us stories about her father—my grandfather—a dedicated healer who had lived in a small village. He concocted treatments for ailments like spider bites and burns, and he used them to care for the people in his village and from other villages nearby. He didn't charge for these services; he simply wanted to help people. That was his goal: to help others and to try to make their lives better.

I was inspired by that story. As a child growing up in India, I had always aspired to be an engineer, but in the moment that I heard that story, I decided that I would become a doctor. I attended medical school in India, and in 1992, I was selected for a residency at the All India Institute of Medical Sciences. Then, in 1993, I came to the United States to finish my residency at Mount Sinai in New York. Afterward I relocated to Florida, where there was an acute need for physicians, and I went to work for another doctor, whom I'll call "Dr. K."

Dr. K. was a brilliant visionary, but he lacked the practical business and operational skills to execute on his practice's vision. For example, at one point he brought *forty* new physicians into one office all at once. As you can likely imagine, he just didn't have the patient volume, nor was he able to develop it fast enough, to keep the considerable overheard of all these provider salaries from pushing him over the financial edge and into bankruptcy. By watching Dr. K., I learned the importance of maintaining a firm handle on the business and financial aspects of the practice, and

v

why strong operational systems and controls are required to help any practice thrive.

While this was happening at Dr. K.'s office, another physician in our county, whom I'll call "Dr. O.," opened a practice of his own. He was ambitious and secured a contract to take all the ER calls at a local hospital. That first year he worked incredibly hard, earning $400,000 for his efforts. So what did he do? He hired a new physician for the second year, and had him take over the ER contract, effectively allowing Dr. O. to stop seeing patients. Well, you can probably guess what happened next. Dr. O.'s patients shifted their loyalties to the new physician or simply left the practice. The new doctor was unhappy and resentful because he was seeing all the patients and he couldn't see how Dr. O. was adding any value. Soon enough, the vast majority of Dr. O.'s patients went elsewhere, and his practice ground to a halt. Yet all of this would have been totally avoidable if Dr. O. had just had a better map for how to mature his practice before he stepped out of the direct clinical treatment of patients.

I have one more story to share with you about a third local doctor, a talented gastroenterologist, who started his practice around this same time as the other doctors I've mentioned. I'll call him "Dr. R." His approach to scaling his practice was quite different from both that of Dr. K. and that of Dr. O. Dr. R. set about personally seeing as many patients as he possibly could. Since he was a very skilled practitioner, he soon had a long waiting list. To handle all this demand, he set a rigorous schedule for himself: His first appointment every day was at six o'clock in the morning, and his last one finished at around eight or even nine o'clock at night. If that sounds draining, that's because it was. Twenty years later, Dr. R. is still working that same grueling schedule, and it is wearing away at him.

Not long ago, Dr. R. threw out his back and required surgery. But with his practice so reliant on his personal efforts, simply taking the necessary time off for his own procedure and recovery brought him to the brink of disaster.

I learned from all of these examples, and though each doctor had his strengths, each one also taught me a bit about what *not* to do.

In 2001, after buying what was left of Dr. K.'s bankrupt practice, I, along with my wife—who is also a primary-care physician—founded Access Health Care in a space that had previously housed an Ace Hardware store. I won't say that we had precisely no idea what we were doing since we had observed these others doctors' mistakes and knew not to repeat them. But we didn't know a whole lot; that's for sure. Back then I didn't have the map you have in this book. I didn't know how to build out our core practice systems and controls, how to grow a management team and integrate new providers, nor did I know how to create a practice culture to keep our systems and team in alignment. I had to figure that out on my own through painful, time-consuming, and expensive trial and error.

One thing we did have was a vision. We set our sights on becoming a full-service practice that would improve care by bringing specialists together under one roof. We envisioned enhanced communication among providers in order to better serve patients. We planned to provide key services, like stress tests and lab work, in-house in order to save patients the hassle of driving around town. And doctors would share back-of-the-house administrative support in order to reduce overhead.

It would be nice to say that our practice simply grew and thrived from that point on, but, of course, that's not what happened at all. We grew in fits and starts, with plenty of mistakes along the way. Today, Access Health Care is a $164-million medical company with eighty-three offices serving 66,000 patients. We employ a staff of 900, including 177 physicians and providers. All of this started out of that old Ace Hardware store location.

Looking back at all our experiences in growing Access and observing my colleagues, I realize that while any doctor can transform his or her practice into a thriving, fulfilling, and profitable venture, most won't. Most physicians I know simply haven't invested the time, attention, and money to develop their business perspectives and skills to be a powerful complement to their clinical skills. As a result, they work harder and harder, under an ever-greater load of stress and anxiety.

But you are different. By getting this book and reading it, you've shown that you've got a hungry mind and you're eager to pick up practical ideas and a proven structure for growing your practice and enjoying an improved quality of life.

I first met David Finkel back in 2015, when my attorney, Alan Gassman (you may have noticed his name listed as one of the coauthors of this book), gave me a copy of David's best seller, *SCALE*. At that time I had been working with Alan as my practice and individual attorney for over thirty-three years, and had learned to trust his suggestions. So when he gave me the book, of course I read it.

The book was fantastic, but my complaint was that he hadn't written it seventeen years earlier, when I first started Access.

Over the past several years, I've enjoyed getting to know David and teaching workshops with him. We have collaborated on how to best apply his structured methodology to grow a business specifically within the world of medicine.

Out of that collaboration came this book, which I know you're going to love, by the way. It's like having a clear map to help you grow your practice by avoiding the common pitfalls that trip up so many other physicians. This map will save you years of time as you go straight to the proven steps and successful strategies to run your practice.

This is essentially the book I wish I had been given seventeen years ago when I started my own practice. Not only would it have saved me millions of dollars in missteps and years of time, but also—and more important—it would have relieved me of so much of the doubt and uncertainty I'd felt because of all the conflicting business advice I had received over the years.

Sure, I'd been lucky to have been able to learn from the failures of my former employer and other local physicians because these examples kept me from making certain mistakes. But if there had been a book to provide me with a clear map for how to accomplish what I wanted to do—a book like the one you're holding in your hands—it would have made my job far easier.

Consider this book your personal guide for spelling out exactly how to build the medical practice you envision. I assure you that it's well within your reach if only you apply the map that's in this book. Congratulations on taking the first step.

—Dr. Pariksith Singh
Spring Hill, Florida

D o you own your practice, or does your practice own you?

We know that's a blunt way to start a business book, but our experiences working with thousands of physicians has taught us that you appreciate candor and directness.

So, have you built an owner-independent practice, or, rather, have you created a job for yourself? If you don't show up at the office tomorrow morning, will patients still be cared for, with consults and exams held and procedures performed? Or will your practice grind to a halt?

We've observed a troubling pattern among physicians in private practice—and our guess is that this pattern is quite familiar to you. It may well be the reason you opened this book.

In our combined seventy-one years working in primary care, coaching doctors on the business side of their practice, and providing legal counsel to medical groups and individual physicians, we've known far too many doctors who have seen their lives consumed by their medical practices. These are doctors who forfeited time with family, their passion for medicine, and nearly their sanity in order to devote sixty, seventy, and even eighty hours a week to their work. At the same time, these doctors didn't necessarily see the financial rewards they'd expected from all that hard work. They made a fine living, yes, but their medical practices hadn't yet achieved the all-out financial success to which they'd aspired—even as they worked harder and harder.

That's why this book begins with an invitation. If the practice you've built has become more of a chore than a joy, where you still show up every day because it supports you and your family, but the pressure and strain of everything on your shoulders, combined with the long hours, have worn away much of what you used to love about the practice of medicine, then this book is for you. If you've ever dreamed of more time away from your practice to spend with your family and on your other passions, and you want to have this time freedom without sacrificing income and practice stability, then this book is an invitation directly to you.

It's an invitation to grow your medical practice and earn more *while working less*. We're guessing that sounds like a fanciful dream, but in the pages ahead you'll read about Dr. Park, who decided to take a methodical approach to building his pain-management practice—and he can now take six months off *every single year*.

You'll also read about Dr. Landon, a solo-practitioner plastic surgeon who was working sixty to seventy hours a week with no end in sight—until he began to make certain key changes at his practice to shorten his working hours while dramatically improving his practice's profitability.

You'll read about Dr. Challa, a highly successful gastroenterologist who has gotten incredible results by applying the strategies and structured map you'll learn in this book to his regional medical group of twenty-three providers.

And you'll read about Dr. Hamil, a bariatric surgeon who shaved ten hours off her work week while growing her practice's profitability by a whopping 40 percent.

These physicians don't have magical powers, and there are many others just like them who have employed some version of the same thing. They all did it by using the structured blueprint that you'll find in this book. We invite you to seize this blueprint and use it to improve your practice and your life.

In Part One, you'll read about the four essential steps that will help you both build your medical practice and reclaim your personal freedom. You'll learn a world-class approach to time management, how to develop the essential business systems to efficiently run your practice, and how to draft the Action Plan that will guide your practice's future.

Then, in Part Two, we'll introduce you to what we call the six "practice accelerators": practical yet powerful strategies for accelerating your practice, from building a phenomenally efficient team to growing revenue while eliminating unnecessary expenses to enlisting expert guidance when you need it.

Essentially, what this book gives you is a proven map that you can follow to grow your practice and increase your personal freedom.

Everything you read in this book has been tested and validated. These are the same strategies that Dr. Singh has used to scale his family-medicine practice into 83 locations with 177 medical providers. Over the past decade David has taught this same methodology to build and scale owner-independent medical practices to thousands of medical groups across North America, and the results his business-coaching clients have enjoyed prove that the concepts, strategies, and tools in this book are transferable and get results. That's why this book is an invitation to you to embark on a journey to a more vibrant, stable practice that is a joy to own.

We're certain that you'll find the strategies in this book to be astonishingly powerful, as Dr. Park, Dr. Landon, Dr. Challa, Dr. Hamil, and many more physicians will tell you. But if you're still not quite certain that this book is for you, consider the following: If the practice you've built has become a draining routine in which you still show up every day only because it supports you and your family—if the pressure, the strain, and the responsibility on your shoulders, combined with the long hours, have eaten away the joy you used to take in practicing medicine—then this book is for you.

If you crave freedom, and if you want your practice to be strong enough to operate smoothly—*independent* of your daily presence at the office—then this book is for you.

If you're simply looking for a proven model to scale your practice, then this book is for you.

If you have the courage to look unflinchingly at the true facts of what you've built, and to take active steps to build an owner-independent practice, then this book is for you.

This invitation marks the starting point. It's the beginning of your building a better, stronger, more profitable practice. So let's not delay another moment, the time is *now*.

FREE Medical Practice Success Tool Kit ($1,375 Value)

Because we know how important executing on these ideas is to help you enjoy the growth and freedom you want, we created a special website with a complete tool kit to help you and your staff apply what you'll learn in this book and get faster results. This free value-add for readers like you includes downloadable PDF versions of the strategy and system-creation tools you'll be introduced to in this book, along with dozens of valuable training videos and other tools to help you grow your practice and get your life back. To get immediate access to these tools, just visit **www.GrowMyMedicalPractice.com**. (See Appendix A for full details.)

PART ONE

Four Simple Steps to Grow Your Medical Practice and Get Your Life Back

Step One:
Make Building an
Owner-Independent
Practice a Stated Goal

Dr. Landon was a successful surgeon with a sterling reputation and a highly profitable practice. When he was in medical school, he learned how to care for patients and help them get the health outcomes they desired. But nowhere in his four years of medical school, six years of general surgery training, and two years of plastic surgery training did he ever learn how to best run a medical practice. So over the two decades after he first opened his surgical practice, he just figured it out as best he could.

By all accounts, he was super successful at it too. He enjoyed a great reputation, and he was making an excellent living. But he was tired—tired of the long days of surgery and tired of fitting in the practice administration on nights and weekends while missing out on time with his family. He was also tired of worrying that if he ever got hurt, his practice could very well fail.

"There was a time, and it wasn't that long ago," Dr. Landon told us, "when, if you had come to me and asked if I could scale the practice, I would have been concerned that the only way for me to do that would be to work longer hours, performing more surgeries and seeing more patients. I was already working sixty to seventy hours a week and didn't want to work more. More than just the hours, however, I didn't like the fact that I had all these people—from my family, to my staff, to my patients—counting on me. If I got hurt, or wanted to take some time away from the practice to compete in a triathlon, the practice would suffer. The business revenue was so dependent on me alone, as the only operating surgeon, and there was no end in sight."

3

To the world, Dr. Landon was a smiling, seven-figure surgeon who had it all under control, but inside he craved a way to reduce his practice's reliance on him. He didn't see how that would ever be possible, though, and so he felt trapped.

Does Dr. Landon's story sound familiar?

According to the Physicians Foundation's 2016 Survey of America's Physicians, *80 percent* of physicians are overextended or at maximum capacity. That survey also found that nearly *half* (49 percent) of all doctors say that they "always" or "often" experience feelings of burnout. The average number of hours worked by U.S. physicians has now inched up to fifty-three per week, with many working seventy hours or more.

How many hours a week on average do you work? The number may be far higher than you think when you add in the email messages handled from home at odd hours and calls taken on nights and weekends, not to mention the time you spend thinking and worrying about your practice when you're away from it.

Are you enjoying the practice you've built? Or, somewhere along the way, did it turn into more of a grind? Have you been able to build a profitable practice that lets you take time away from the office to spend with your family? It's one thing to earn a healthy six- or seven-figure income, but if your practice requires you to fuel that income through long hours and high pressure through your own personal medical production, then not only is your practice vulnerable to something happening to you, but it is also always going to be limited. After all, there are only so many hours in the day and so many patients you can see and procedures that you can personally perform.

This is why the first step to building the practice you dream of owning is to make building an owner-independent practice a *stated* goal of your practice.

We know what you're thinking: *It's just not possible to build an owner-independent practice. My patients wouldn't want to see anybody else. My staff would be upset.* When we first talk with physicians about what's in this book—about the fact that they really *can* build an owner-independent practice—they don't believe it's possible. More specifically, they don't believe it's possible for them. Often they've seen *other* physicians do it. Sure, Dr. Singh can do it with his 177-provider family practice. Maybe they even know someone like Dr. Park—who you'll read about in this book—who works just six months out of the year and takes six months off, all while running a multimillion-dollar practice. But every doctor we know, when they first consider the idea of turning their own practice into one that's owner independent, believes that their particular circumstances make it impossible. And it's this kind of automatic, conditioned thinking that keeps them trapped.

We'll be honest. There are some important reasons why, from where you're sitting, the idea of turning your practice into one that's owner independent looks and *feels* impossible:

- **The stacked deck.** The practice of medicine has become a treadmill. The entire economic model is built on the expectation that you will see patient after patient after patient from daybreak until after the sun sets. In some ways, your work has become a commodity, a numbers game that's all about volume. There seems to be no way out. The more you work, the more patients you see, the more your practice is dependent on your personal production for its success. With that for a backdrop, it's no wonder that it's hard to imagine your practice humming along nicely without you. In fact, your practice may be so dependent on your around-the-clock devotion that your staff may be terrified of something happening to you. If a bus hit you tomorrow, they'd be out of a job in an instant. It's a scary situation.

- **The "competency trap."** We'll be frank here and acknowledge that *you are exceedingly competent*. In college you posted the grades and board scores you needed to get into medical school, and in medical school you absorbed and mastered a staggering amount of information. All told, you've had the better part of a decade or more in professional training, after which you went on to establish your own practice—which you built, one patient at a time, on the foundation of your competence as a physician. Such competence is normally something to celebrate, but in a sense, it's now working against you. You're so darn competent that it's hard to let other people handle tasks that you know you can perform better. You may very well find it excruciating to watch a member of your staff do something less well than you know it can be done. You may feel constantly compelled to step in, to handle any and every little job in order to make sure it's executed properly. But the more you do, the more you have to keep doing. And over time, the accumulation of myriad responsibilities becomes a heavier and heavier burden to carry.

▪ **Controlitis.** *Controlitis* is the inflammation of your control gland—and boy, do we understand! We're a bunch of control freaks ourselves who run over a dozen different companies with annual revenues of over $1 billion. At various times we've found ourselves saying, "If you want something done right, you've got to do it yourself." Business owners generally tend to be control freaks, and physicians who own their own practices tend to be control freaks twice over. We get it. But recognize the high price you are paying for your urge to control every detail of your practice. We're not going to tell you to just abdicate responsibility, but rather, to build on a stable base of sound business systems, a talented and well-trained team, and a culture that helps ensure that your team properly handles any ambiguous situation that arises.

▪ **Lack of business training.** In all that training, they never taught you practice management. There's yet another way that the deck is stacked against you. In all your years of professional training, from medical school to residency to specialty training, you likely had somewhere around zero hours of instruction on the business of running a medical practice. This implicit bias in medical training—the bias of not talking about business or profit or anything related to it—probably didn't seem like a problem at the time; after all, you weren't expecting a curriculum in business management. You went to school to become a doctor, and that was precisely the education you received. But if you pause and think about it, this situation is absolutely crazy. A medical practice is a complex business; it sure isn't just going to run itself. And yet doctors typically receive no training at all in how to build a practice that not only delivers great medical care but is also financially viable, never mind highly efficient and scalable.

Maybe that's the reason that more and more doctors are leaving private practice to become employed physicians. Over the past decade, the number of employed physicians has grown by a whopping 20 percent. Those doctors, like you, never had any training in business management, and they ultimately determined they couldn't run a practice and practice medicine. Doing both is an impressive feat.

Happily, we're about to make that impressive feat a whole lot easier. We're going to help you turn your practice into a successful business that's owner independent. You'll only regret that you didn't do it sooner.

Three Excuses That Are Holding You Back

We've met a lot of doctors who believed that others could build an owner-independent practice, but not themselves. What we've discovered is that their excuses are remarkably similar.

Excuse #1: "I can't afford it."

Many doctors initially think only in terms of what it will cost them to invest in the staff, systems, and outside help they need to grow and develop their practice to be owner independent. For them, the decision is skewed because they're looking at the cost of the investment while ignoring the cost of the status quo.

Let's go back to Dr. Landon's story. Like so many other doctors, Dr. Landon was so mired in being a provider of medical care that he wasn't able to step back and view his practice accurately. One of the first things he discovered when he began working with David's business-coaching company was that one part of his medical practice was losing quite a bit of money every year. We'll get into the details later, but the first simple changes that he made fixed this issue and resulted in an annual increase in profit of $250,000. At the same time, he reduced his own schedule by ten hours a week.

Remember, there is a cost to the status quo. When done right, moving toward a more owner-independent practice will free up this trapped cash for better and higher uses in the practice.

Excuse #2: "I don't have the time."

No doctor initially feels like he or she has extra time to devote to scaling his or her practice. Instead, doctors feel strained to capacity and maxed out. We call this "death by a thousand cuts." Of course you're overwhelmed, because you're constantly putting out fires: One of your patients has a unique demand, someone on your staff has a personal issue, a referring physician asks you for a favor, there's a problem with a key vendor, a nurse's assistant puts in her two weeks' notice. A hundred things like this can happen every month, and it saps your time as well as your energy and passion for the work. The actual practice of medicine may have even become your escape hatch because it's the only time you're not mired in management problems.

So we'll be very clear: You don't need to work more hours. We will never ask you to work more hours. We'll never ask you to work longer hours because building your practice solely by you personally seeing more patients and performing more procedures is one of the core reasons why your practice is so reliant on you on the first place. Instead, we'll show you how to grow your practice by working less while getting your practice to produce more.

This means designing and implementing better workflows and systems; growing, developing, and engaging your team; and making and executing on better strategic choices in the management and leadership of your practice. Together, these simple changes will not only put you on the path to higher profits, but, more importantly, they'll also lead you to a practice you once again love owning.

It has been our direct experience in coaching hundreds of doctors that if you're serious about making things better, you will see a sizable change in a very short time. A quick review of David's coaching clients shows that within six to twelve months of getting started, you'll feel like you can breathe again. You'll feel like you're in control of your practice, rather than your practice controlling you.

It's a Progression, Not an On/Off Switch

As you'll come to learn, building an owner-independent business is a progression, not a light switch you suddenly flip on one day. It's not a binary yes/no, but rather a spectrum along which you gradually progress over the course of several years.

The critical shift is from seeing yourself as a *producer* for your practice—treating patients and performing procedures—to seeing yourself as the *builder* of a business that will do all this without you. You're only a temporary producer until you can build the business depth that can replace you.

Let's return once again to Dr. Landon's story. It would be easy for him, as a successful surgeon, to see himself as the key driver that propels his business—the one irreplaceable ingredient without which the practice would wither and die. Within six months of working with David's coaching team, however, Dr. Landon reduced his working hours in the practice by ten per week. He also increased his operating profit by $250,000 a year, and climbing. And he is starting to feel as though there is a pathway for him to scale the practice and get his life back. Here's how he put it:

I had twelve years of advanced medical training to become a surgeon, yet I received no training in how to run a successful medical practice. I had to learn by trial and error. Now, with the support and training of my business coach, I'm finally getting that business training. I'm working fewer hours, and actually getting home before the sun sets, which is a real gift. Best of all, I can see the practice becoming stronger and less reliant on me bit by bit each quarter.

Remember, this work is a progression, not an on/off switch. You'll make headway and have temporary reversals, and at times, progress will feel slow, almost as if you're pushing uphill. This is normal. But if you persevere, if you stay the course that we'll lay out for you in this book, you will enjoy greater profits and an improved quality of life. Looking back at the considerable progress he has already achieved—and having watched other physicians struggle with the same challenges—Dr. Landon shared the following:

> It's a sad fact that the majority of doctors I know end up twenty years into their practice feeling trapped and stuck. Sure, they make a great living, but they have to give up so much of their time and life to do it. Maybe you can't make your practice operate completely independently from you, but you can make it much better than it is now. I've seen what a difference working in a structured way on my practice over the past six months has made for me personally. The practice runs more smoothly, it's more profitable, and our staff is happier. Stop making excuses and take that first step.

Excuse #3: "What will my staff say?"

We've worked with many doctors who were terrified of telling their staff that they're planning to work less and eventually make the practice owner independent. Their fear is that what their staff will hear is, "I'm planning on working a whole lot less by having you work a whole lot more." But this simply isn't accurate.

What we are coaching you to do is to build a more vibrant practice that leverages the talents of your team to produce great-quality medical care for your patients, while at the same time weaning your business off of its crippling dependence on you. Done the way that we describe in this book, this means greater opportunity for your team to grow professionally and contribute more. They'll be able to enjoy more autonomy and have a bigger impact on the practice. While this will likely afford them an opportunity to earn more, the biggest benefit to your staff is their own professional growth and the enhanced stability of working for a practice that is no longer one car accident away from everyone losing his or her job. Sounds like a pretty good deal to us.

The truth is that there will always be excuses. The timing will never seem just right, for this or for anything. Rather than waiting for the perfect moment, you've got to decide that your starting point is today—right now. Make building an owner-independent practice a *stated* goal of your practice.

Building a Level Three Owner-Independent Practice

A medical practice doesn't become owner independent overnight, of course. Rather, it's a process that unfolds over time (see Figure 1.1). What follows is a quick overview of the three-level model for scaling your practice. In later chapters, we'll dive progressively deeper into the specific steps and refinements for progressing through these levels to reach your destination: a "Level Three" owner-independent practice.

Level One: The Start-up—No Control, No Freedom

You've just launched your practice. At this point, you have no freedom because you're working long hours to get things going. You're scrambling to get those initial patients and to figure out how your practice will operate. Will you ever bring in enough patients to be profitable? Will you have the cash to meet payroll next week? Doctors at Level One are usually filled with a mixture of doubts and dreams, fears and ambitions. They work long hours in an attempt to turn their vision for their practice into a sustainable enterprise.

Level Two: The Owner-Reliant Practice—Control, but No Freedom

You're practicing medicine full time and you've built up a practice that works—as long as you are present each day to keep it working. You make most of the decisions. Your efforts bring in the majority of the new patients, and you likely perform most of the important work. You are in full control. Sure, you have people to help, but they're there to do just that—help—not to lead or take ownership.

You have the control, but along with that control, you also have long hours and the sense that all the decisions, all the risks, and all the responsibility rest on your shoulders. Every day you have to keep going because if you stop, it all ends. You have control, but no real freedom.

Level Three: The Owner-Independent Practice—Total Freedom

You're the owner of a practice that whistles along without requiring your day-to-day presence. You've got the right team and systems in place to ensure that your practice's success is independent of you. While you may still see patients, you've got other providers who provide core medical services; your own production, while a real positive, is no longer essential for your practice to be successful. For you, working has become a choice, not an obligation or a requirement. At this point you can continue to scale the practice, or transition to own it passively.

Your Responsibility to Serve

In the pages ahead you'll see how you really can work less while producing more. You will learn that you can break the chain between one unit of time worked and one unit of value created. You'll do this by applying your time differently—by devoting yourself to strategic decisions, rather than performing rote tasks; by growing and developing the systems and team to treat patients, rather than just rushing from one exam room to the next all day long. In this way you'll begin to produce more (much more) for every hour you work.

And we will go so far as to say you have a *responsibility* to break the chain between one unit of time and one unit of value. Right now, you spend ten hours caring for patients and, in so doing, you produce ten

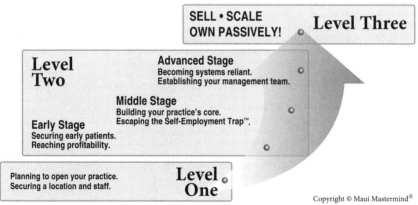

Figure 1.1: Level Three Map™

hours' worth of value. This book is about finding and implementing ways to create *thousands* of hours of patient value for every ten hours you work—an exponential increase. We believe that you have a responsibility to pursue such dramatic improvement because of the importance of what you do.

After all, you didn't go into medicine so that you could go through the motions of being a doctor. You went into medicine because you believe in helping your patients and serving them through the care that you provide. If you remain stuck in your current model, in which you simply can't do more because you're limited by the number of hours in a day, then there are patients who will miss out. There are patients who would benefit from the services your practice provides, but at this rate, they'll never know your office exists, and even if they did call for an appointment, you might not be able to fit them in. We're about to change that.

Right now is the only time to get started. Today is the day to create a new beginning so that you can enjoy the better ending you deserve. Waiting will only make the task more difficult. In the words of Nike, "Just do it!"

2

Step Two:
Reclaim Your Best Time

Nine years ago, when we first started working with Dr. Padda, a physician who practices in St. Louis, Missouri, he thought the best use of his time was performing surgery, specifically the pain-intervention spinal procedures in which he was a world-class expert. But the more he took the concepts of time mastery and business growth to heart, the clearer it became that, though very lucrative, surgery hours were not the best use of his time after all.

So what *was* the best use of his time? As you'll learn from this book, time spent making strategic decisions, hiring and empowering key team members, building core systems, engaging in crucial negotiations, and creating valuable strategic relationships are the most valuable activities for one's practice.

Here's how Dr. Padda described himself before he began to take this new approach to time management:

I was a surgeon with a thriving pain-management practice. At the time I first started using David's time-mastery strategies, I was already stretched to the maximum, running a dozen different businesses, from a medical billing company to several commercial real estate projects and even a few restaurants.

Overextended and searching for a better way, Dr. Padda began making certain crucial, strategic changes—which you'll read about in a moment—to the way he structured and leveraged his time. Within a couple months, he started to notice a difference in how much he was able to accomplish. His sense of stress began to diminish.

Today, Dr. Padda owns seven medical clinics and employs hundreds of people. Here's how he explains the changes that have taken place at his practice and in his life after a couple years of utilizing our time-mastery strategies:

> These ideas helped me radically upgrade my use of time, and within two years, I increased my personal income by an additional $1 million per year. I still use these strategies, and, to this day, find them just as useful and profitable.

Though Dr. Padda is clearly an outlier in terms of how much he has been able to accomplish, his example shows how powerful the time-mastery program in this chapter can truly be. You're about to discover a life-changing system for reclaiming some of your best time to reinvest in the high-value work that will actually grow your practice.

What you've done up until now is squeezed little bits of practice management into the corners of your day. You fit it in around the core of practicing medicine. But the truth is, that doesn't really work, and it's definitely not going to work as you start to scale your practice and move toward owner independence.

You're now going to need real blocks of time—initially, as few as two hours (or more) every week—to take off your physician's hat and put on your practice owner's hat to work on higher-value activities to grow your practice. The time-mastery strategies that you're about to learn will free up much more than just these two hours. In fact, these strategies will fundamentally alter the way you use your working time, by allowing you to implement a structure that consistently provides weekly and daily blocks in which to do your highest-value work. Let's get started.

Time-Mastery Strategy #1:
Build Your Personal "Time Value Matrix"

To dramatically upgrade the way you use your time, the first step is to identify what you do that truly creates the most value for your practice. If you've read some management literature, you may have come across the Pareto Principle, also known as the 80/20 Rule. The Pareto Principle says that 20 percent of your actions generate 80 percent of your results (high value) and the other 80 percent of your actions generate the other 20 percent of your results (low value).

We're going to use this distinction to define your low-value work and separate it from your high-value work, and then we're going to use it as a model for creating massive value, independent of the number of hours you put in. If you take the 20 percent of your actions that generate 80 percent of your results and apply the same distinction a second time, then 20 percent of that 20 percent produces 80 percent of 80 percent of your results. That means 4 percent of your efforts generate 64 percent of your results. And if you apply this distinction yet again, it means that around 1 percent (20 percent of 20 percent of 20 percent) generates about 50 percent of your results. That's right; just a fraction of your highest-leverage work produces a full *half* of all the value you create.

We applied this idea to create what we call the Time Value Matrix™ (see Figure 2.1), with which you can quickly and accurately quantify the value of four distinct types of time:

D Time is the 80 percent of your work that is unleveraged and generates just 20 percent of your total return. We call this the "80 Percent Mass."

C Time is the leveraged 20 percent that produces 80 percent of your results. We call this "Leveraged Time."

B Time is the highly focused 4 percent that generates 64 percent of your results. We call this time the "4 Percent Sweet Spot."

A Time is the top of the pyramid—the "Magic 1 Percent." Fifty percent of your results come from A Time.

TIME VALUE MATRIX™

	INPUT	OUTPUT	RELATIVE VALUE
A time Magic 1%	1%	50%	200 XD
B time 4% Sweet Spot	4%	64%	64 XD
C time Leveraged 20%	20%	80%	16 XD
D time 80% Mass	80%	20%	1 XD

Copyright © Maui Mastermind®

Figure 2.1: The Time Value Matrix

It's important to note that one person's D-level activity may be another person's A- or B-level activity; it's all relative. For example, one of Dr. Singh's D-level activities is ordering supplies for his practice—but there are people who work for him who have this as one of their C-level activities. Your A-, B-, C-, and D-level activities are comparable only to you, not to other people.

Let's apply this distinction to your own work. To get you started, Dr. Singh has provided some examples. Take a few minutes as you read through this section to record on paper your A-, B-, C-, and D-level activities. If you would like to use our Time Value Matrix Tool, just go to **www.GrowMyMedicalPractice.com** and download our free PDF tool.

D Time: The 80 percent that produces only 20 percent of your total return. Here are some of Dr. Singh's "D Time" activities:

- Fixing the Wi-Fi in his office
- Writing low-level email messages
- Scanning documents into his electronic filing system
- Scheduling patients

Now list five of your "D Time" activities:

1. _____

2. _____

3. _____

4. _____

5. _____

C Time: The leveraged 20 percent that produces 80 percent of your results. Here are some of Dr. Singh's "C Time" activities:

- Treating patients
- Delegating to his assistant
- Making low-level financial decisions
- Dictating treatment notes

Now list five of your "C Time" activities:

1. _____

2. _____

3. _____

4. _____

5. _____

B Time: The highly focused "4 Percent Sweet Spot" that generates 64 percent of your results. Here are some of Dr. Singh's "B Time" activities:

- Giving a keynote address

- Coaching his management team to be better leaders

- Reviewing his company's quarterly progress

- Holding his management team accountable for their deliverables

- Instituting a systemic solution to a recurring problem

- Spending at least a few minutes briefly conferring with legal and tax advisors to help assure that significant threats that might otherwise apply are best handled

Now list five of your "B Time" activities:

1. _____

2. _____

3. _____

4. _____

5. _____

A Time: The "Magic 1 Percent" that generates more than 50 percent of your total results. Here are some of Dr. Singh's "A Time" activities:

- Designing his practice's pricing model

- Making executive-level hiring and firing decisions

- Getting expert input on core issues and opportunities from his legal, tax, and business advisors
- Meeting with key joint venture partners to secure high-value, win-win strategic partnerships

Now list five of your "A Time" activities:

1. _____

2. _____

3. _____

4. _____

5. _____

When you start to make this distinction between A, B, C, and D Time as a matter of habit, you'll find yourself starting to upgrade the type of work you do—by doing more A and B, and less D. And we can promise you this: You'll find the results to be amazing.

If the distinction between A and B Time feels fuzzy right now, don't worry. What matters now is that you understand in your gut that A and B Time is *qualitatively* a magnitude more valuable for your practice than your C or D Time. This is the basis of how you will grow your practice without working more hours. You don't need more hours; you just need to regularly upgrade a few hours of your D Time into A- and B-level uses.

It's also important to understand that what you currently list as an A- or B-level activity will change over time. For example, if right now a marketing activity that brings in a dozen new patients is an A-level activity for you, make sure that in six to twelve months, you've increased the value you create for your practice so that this activity is pushed down to a B-level activity. Or, if currently your personally performing a specific high-revenue procedure is a B-level activity, work on developing your provider team and your practice so that in twelve to eighteen months, that becomes a C-level activity for you.

Your core time strategy is to free up more A and B Time by reducing your D Time tasks. The key is to make sure that the time you do free up actually goes into A- and B-level uses, and is not wasted on other D-level junk. Generally, A- and B-level activities are where you step out of the day-to-day practice of medicine and do the higher-level work that actually improves the practice's capacity to grow.

It might seem surprising to you, as it was for Dr. Padda, that your time spent treating patients—and even performing $1,000-an-hour surgery—is C-level work. This is important to understand: C Time can provide you with a great income, but you'll always have to work exceptionally hard to earn it, and it will likely always be dependent on your personal participation. This is the trap that catches most doctors.

Now, instead of trying to grow your practice by working more hours and seeing more patients, you're going to upgrade your use of time. That will allow you to generate huge business breakthroughs while working fewer hours. Trading time for dollars is the paradigm of a Level Two practice; upgrading your use of time to create more with less is how you soar to Level Three.

So here's the big question: How can you have more A and B Time? The answer is to fundamentally alter the way you structure your day and your week, which is exactly what you'll do by applying the next four time-mastery strategies.

Time-Mastery Strategy #2:
Apply the Four Ds to Your D Time

To "find" the time to devote to A- and B-level work, focus first on your D-level activities. That may seem counterintuitive, but, in fact, this is the best place to start. Not only do you, by definition, spend a lot more time on the D-level stuff, but it's the easiest place to make changes, because the consequences of dropping those activities are small.

So start by listing all the D-level activities you do on a weekly basis. We even recommend keeping a time log for a week or two so you can spot all the time wasted on low-value D-level work. Once you've identified all those D-level activities, you can apply the following "Four Ds" to get them off your plate:

The Four Ds

1. **Delete it.** Some D-level activities just plain shouldn't be done by anyone. Look at the action item and ask yourself what the consequences would be if no one did it. If the consequences would be small, then consider just crossing it off your list altogether.

2. **Delegate it.** Maybe it's a task that needs to get done, but not necessarily by you. Hand it off to your assistant, a staff member, or a vendor. Anytime you can hand off a D-level activity to someone,

you free up both your time and your focus to do more valuable work.

3. **Defer it.** Maybe this task needs to be done, and done by you, but should it happen right now? Sometimes delaying the action is the smartest choice.

4. **Design it out.** If you find yourself handling a recurring D-level activity over and over, instead of doing it, improve the process or system to keep the task from coming up in the first place.

Take the example of Dr. Scheiner, a renowned laser eyelid and facial plastic surgeon. Considering the number of procedures Dr. Scheiner performs each year, he cumulatively used to spend hundreds of hours giving preoperative instructions and explanations to his patients. Then one day he "designed it out." He produced a simple, clear, and detailed video that he now shows patients with all the preoperative education and instructions that he used to say over and over and over. After they watch this video, he comes back into the exam room and answers any questions they might have. This saves him many hours each month and gives his patients a better experience.

Other examples of designing it out include redesigning your new-patient paperwork and instructions so that they're easier for patients to understand and complete, with fewer questions for your staff. Or you might consider preempting the five most common new-patient questions by giving them a "quick start" booklet that proactively answers these common questions. Or post an educational video for a subset of your patients online, the way Dr. Scheiner did. You get the idea.

Designing out a recurring activity is the very essence of building a systems-reliant Level Three practice. It simplifies processes and empowers your team to get consistently great results with less and less reliance on you, the owner.

By applying all four Ds—Deleting, Delegating, Deferring, and Designing Out—you're likely to free up at least two hours (or many, many more) *every single week* to reinvest in A- and B-level activities.

Time-Mastery Strategy #3: Take a Focus Day

It's not enough to free up two or more hours each week by clearing the clutter of your D-level work. The next essential step is to fill your newly available time with A- and B-level activities. One way you'll do this is by structuring your week differently; time-mastery strategies #3 and #4 are specifically designed to help you do this. Let's start with a powerful technique that we call "Focus Days and Push Days."

Focus Days are for doing the highest-value activities: your A- and B-level work. On Focus Days, you'll block out a two- to four-hour period of time during which you'll focus on the high-value A- and B-level activities you've identified for your practice (more on what to fill your focus time with in the next chapter). We encourage you to turn off your phone, disconnect from the internet, and close your office door so that you're genuinely free from distractions.

Push Days are for pushing key projects forward one step at a time. This is when you do the "work" of your practice, like treating patients and doing the day-to-day work of operating your practice.

The Focus Days and Push Days technique is powerful precisely because it delivers solid blocks of time for you to do your best work. Up until now you've been fitting the management of your practice into little gaps in your schedule. Focus Days will now give you consistent blocks of time in which to do key strategic work—the work that will move your practice toward Level Three owner independence.

Action Step: Set Aside Your Focus Day

Start by setting aside at least part of one day each week as your Focus Day. Eventually you'll want a full day, but you can start by setting aside as little as a weekly two-hour block. As you continually move D-level activities off your plate and become more efficient, you'll allocate that newly available time to your Focus Day, so that it grows from two hours to, eventually, a full day each week. (TIP: If you're like most doctors, the two hours you set aside for your Focus Day will need to occur first thing in the morning—because if you wait until the afternoon, you'll never get to it.)

Decision Time: What day will you make your Focus Day?

My Focus Day will be _____.

Dr. Singh's Focus Days and Push Days

Every week, Tuesday and Thursday are Dr. Singh's Focus Days. On those days, he engages in his A- and B-level activities, which most often means educating his top-level staff. On a recent Focus Day, he went to one of his hospitals to meet with a team of hospitalists. For Dr. Singh, this is the work that creates the greatest results.

"I have two days each week to spend teaching my providers so that they continue to scale our company vision," says Dr. Singh. "When I'm working with them, I translate the vision of the company and make sure that they're able to flow with it. That is critical work."

You might feel that devoting two full days each week for A- and B-level work is impossible for your schedule—and, at least for now, it may well be out of reach. But you should also know that Dr. Singh still sees a great many patients.

On Mondays, Wednesdays, and Fridays, Dr. Singh sees patients from eight o'clock in the morning until three-thirty in the afternoon—and on each of these days, he sees a total of forty-five patients. How can he do so much in that window of time? He uses mid-level providers and a top-quality front- and back-office staff to support his work and help maximize his efficiency. Then, after seeing patients, he returns to his office for a Prime-Time block of two hours, and uses that time to do higher-value work for his practice.

This schedule is what has made it possible for Dr. Singh to grow Access Health Care into the phenomenal success that it is—and still make it home to enjoy dinner with his family every night.

Time-Mastery Strategy #4:
Schedule a Prime-Time Block on Your Push Days

The second way you'll create blocks of higher-value time to grow your practice is by setting aside a forty-five- to sixty-minute "Prime-Time" block on two or more of your Push Days. During this Prime-Time block, you'll have time to work on one or more of your A- or B-level activities.

Everyone has a certain time in the day when they're at their best. A Prime-Time block is a forty-five-minute to one-hour appointment that you set for yourself at your time of peak effectiveness. That's when you work on only your highest-value items. By blocking out this time as an actual appointment on your calendar, you guarantee yourself at least a few hours more each week to create real value for your practice.

See Figure 2.2 below to see how a Focus Day and Prime-Time blocks might look when you see your weekly schedule. Notice how it regularly blocks out three to four hours each week for you to do higher-value projects for your practice. By blocking out this time first, you crowd out some of the C- and D-level activities that otherwise would dominate your week.

The Real Secret to Unshakable Time Discipline

Most people shudder when they think about a need for greater discipline because they've always associated it with pain and effort. But that isn't accurate. We suggest that you link discipline to two very important positive concepts: accountability and environment.

Mon		Tue		Wed		Thur		Fri	
8	Prime Time	8		8	Prime Time	8		8	Prime Time
9		9	Focus Day	9		9		9	
10		10		10		10		10	
11		11		11		11		11	
12		12		12		12		12	
1		1		1		1		1	
2		2		2		2		2	
3		3		3		3		3	
4		4		4		4	Prime Time	4	
5		5		5		5		5	

Copyright © Maui Mastermind®

Figure 2.2: Weekly Time-Mastery Schedule

Discipline Is One Part Accountability

There is a powerful part of human nature that drives us to seek the esteem of the people we admire. One of the best ways to increase your time discipline is to have a formal accountability structure to someone whose respect you want to earn, and whose opinion of you matters greatly to you. In Chapter 10, you'll read about how to leverage a business coach to perform this essential function.

Who holds you accountable for your actions and decisions within your practice? Who coaches you to help you develop as a business owner? Who helps keep you on track? If you want to build an owner-independent Level Three practice, it's vital to have an accountability structure. And you need this accountability to be formal, not ad hoc or hit-or-miss. Formal means you make regular, timed commitments (i.e., weekly, biweekly, monthly, and/or quarterly), with a structured plan by which you'll report on your results meeting those commitments.

With this approach, no hiding is possible, just the naked truth that you stand up and unflinchingly own. This one element is perhaps the biggest reason David's business-coaching clients grow on average at an annual rate that's five times faster than that of non-clients; they have a structured accountability system that makes it impossible to hide.

If you want to build an owner-independent Level Three business, it's vital to have an accountability structure. Remember, on your own, you are vulnerable. But connected with an advisor team and peer group that can give you feedback and accountability, you are unstoppable.

Discipline Is One Part Environment

Discipline also results from working in a structured environment. By controlling your environment, you'll make it much easier to act in ways that are healthy and profitable for your practice. This means eliminating distractions on your Focus Day and during your Prime-Time blocks. Consider leaving your office for a few hours to go to your local Starbucks. At the very least, turn off your email, office ringer, and cell phone. You might feel like you can simply rely on willpower to resist distractions, but while willpower may be enough to win a sprint, it's rarely sufficient to win a marathon. To win the marathon of building a Level Three business, take control of your environment to ensure it supports your goals each day.

The bottom line is that the real secret of time discipline is to harness the power of accountability—and the human desire that we all feel to be esteemed by the people we respect—*and* control your environment so that you design out your old distractions while creating a workspace that supports you working at your best.

When Dr. Padda implemented the strategies that you just read about, he saw outstanding results. Within two years he had increased his personal income by an additional $1 million per year. He continues to use these strategies today—and he continues to reap the benefits. Now it's your turn.

These time-mastery strategies are also exponentially more effective when you pair them with the strategic-planning tools you'll learn about in the next chapter. We call this the art and science of defining your practice's "fewer, better"—and you'll discover the secrets of how to do just that in the next chapter.

3

Step Three: Determine Your Practice's "Fewer, Better"

D r. Hamil was a top surgeon in her field. She, like her peers, spent her days alternating back and forth between office days, when she took consults and followed up with patients, and surgery days on which she performed a full day of back-to-back cases starting at six o'clock in the morning and finishing at six in the evening.

In the rush of these packed clinical and surgery days, Dr. Hamil had no time to step back and think about the *business* of her practice, let alone be strategic about growing it. She just didn't have the time since she was already working seventy hours a week or more—at least, that was her excuse until she started working with David's business-coaching team.

One of the first things her assigned coach pushed her to do was to block out one two-hour block each week to think about her practice. You may recognize this as the "Focus Day" strategy we shared with you in the last chapter. Pay close attention to how Dr. Hamil leveraged this two-hour weekly block.

The first thing her coach got her to do with her newfound block of time was to perform a "margin analysis," breaking down her surgical cases by payer. What she discovered shocked her. Her in-network insurers were paying between $3,000 and $3,500 for a procedure that out-of-network and private payers reimbursed at $15,000 to $18,000. Same duty of care, same procedure, same time expense, same back-end costs—but one type of payer translated into as much as *six times* greater profit. While Dr. Hamil knew she made more from out-of-network and private payers, she had never taken the time or cleared the mental space to step back from the rush of her practice to look at the business economics of her situation. Her coach pushed her to not only face this uncomfortable reality, but to see the opportunity it presented her.

Dr. Hamil used this insight to be much more strategic about how she had her staff book cases. She made a point of scheduling more out-of-network and private-pay patients in her surgery calendar. At the same time, for philosophical reasons, she still held spots for in-network and Medicare patients; now, though, she was much more intentional about the number of surgical slots she set aside for these types of payers every month.

Through this small change, Dr. Hamil achieved impressive results. She was able to shave ten hours off each work week to spend with her young family, and at the same time, she grew her revenues by 50 percent a year.

With this early victory under her belt, Dr. Hamil continued to take her focus time each week. She used this time to work with her staff on their marketing systems to bring in more out-of-network and private-payer patients, and to later recruit and train a second surgeon for the practice. In fact, we still remember the day when Dr. Hamil joined us for an advanced practice-growth conference we hosted in Florida. She pulled out her iPhone and, beaming, said, "This is my surgery schedule today." It was filled with cases that her new surgeon was performing during the day of the conference.

"Before I began working with you to build my practice the right way, I would have either had to close the office to be here with you, or I just wouldn't have been able to come. Now, here I am with you, but my office and team are doing procedures and helping patients without me there. It's an amazing feeling."

In the last chapter we introduced you to Dr. Padda, the pain-management physician who was able to increase his practice's bottom-line profit by over $1 million per year. His success is so remarkable, in fact, that you might have had trouble imagining exactly how he built a medical practice that could be so superbly profitable without increasing his own workload. To this day, Dr. Padda only works at his practice for thirty-five hours a week.

So let's pull back the curtain a little more, and take a closer look at how Dr. Padda has structured his practice. Over his years in practice, he had observed many other physicians providing services that insurers reimburse at a rate of $90 an hour. Those same physicians would often carry overhead costs of about 50 percent—meaning that their gross profit amounted to just $45 an hour. At $45 hourly, those physicians would only take home around $80,000 a year.

Instead of falling into this trap, Dr. Padda and his team carefully evaluate each type of service for how much net profit it can generate. Then they apply a threshold of $1,600 gross profit per hour; if a type of care can't hit that threshold, his practice will probably not provide it in-house.

Here's one way in which this rule of thumb has informed strategic decision making at his practice. Dr. Padda runs a highly successful pain-management clinic as well as a bariatric program. He could easily add sleep medicine to this suite of services as well. But when Dr. Padda and his team analyzed the financial potential of doing sleep medicine, they found that it wouldn't generate enough revenue to justify adding it to their practice. Instead, when Dr. Padda and his staff of providers identify patients in need of a sleep study, they send those patients to a third party. That third party is one that specializes in sleep medicine, with all the infrastructure and technology to drive down their costs, such that they can generate substantial revenue through that particular service in a way that Dr. Padda can't.

Consider another powerful example of this same type of thinking from a different doctor, David's coaching client Dr. Lara. Dr. Lara ran a successful multi-clinic weight-loss and anti-aging practice. When his business coach did a deep dive with Dr. Lara into the practice's financials, what quickly became clear was that two of his four locations were extremely profitable, and these two locations were carrying the two other marginally profitable offices. By facing this unpleasant truth, Dr. Lara and his coach were able to map out a strategy to close one location, freeing up hundreds of thousands of dollars, and work to shift the patients to the other clinics, which resulted in a rapid increase to the bottom line.

These changes had a big impact on the overall practice, but that's not even the most important part. Collectively, making these changes took fewer than three hours a week of Dr. Lara's direct time over a twelve-month period. Yet, thanks to the changes he made, the practice is more profitable than ever. At the same time, he has regained a full day each week from active clinical work for his Focus Day, and he spends that time on continued work to grow the practice.

In just the same way that key changes brought such great results for Dr. Hamil and Dr. Lara, making a few key changes to your practice will have a major impact for you too. This chapter is all about *how*. How do you consistently get your practice to invest its time, talent, attention, and money into the right things in the face of so many competing demands?

The answer is by first pinpointing the highest-leverage places on which to focus your practice-building efforts, then turning those leverage points into a clearly written, one-page Action Plan. With this Action Plan in hand, you and your team will then execute on these fewer, better priorities to help speed growth while using a minimum of your personal time and effort. This is the same methodology that David has used with his business-coaching clients for over a decade to such powerful effect.

In this chapter, you'll learn how to use a powerful strategic structure for your practice that specifies your Focus Areas and maps out exactly how you'll scale—and, eventually, how you'll make your practice owner independent.

Ready?

A Better Structure to Map Out Your Practice's Growth

It's time to determine your growth strategy and then reduce that strategy into a series of rolling, one-page quarterly Action Plans that help you execute and get results. In this chapter, we'll walk you through a concrete, structured process to do exactly that.

Your strategic plan is the map that directs your focus to the fewer, better priorities that will allow you to grow and mature your practice. It prompts you to look at the big picture: What really matters to you? Where are you committed to going? How can you meaningfully and accurately track your progress? Your strategic plan also helps you prioritize and intelligently allocate your company's resources of time, talent, attention, and money to best advantage. Finally, your strategic plan helps align your team members around a big picture so they can better manage their own responsibilities and make greater contributions to the real needs of the practice. That sounds pretty good, doesn't it?

As you execute on your plan, you've got to strike a working balance between change and momentum. Change says, "Hey, let's question our focus and radically redesign our approach." Change is essential to keeping your practice fresh and relevant in the marketplace. It allows you to nimbly seize opportunities. But change also stresses out your team and puts increased demands on your limited resources. It often causes you to scrap existing systems, products, and infrastructure as they become dated. Transitioning from a static idea to a moving, producing idea in the market demands extra energy (read: time, effort, and money).

Meanwhile, momentum says, "I'm working. Feed me! Support my success and build on my breakthroughs." It leverages your known winners and doubles down on your strongest successes by scaling and optimizing what has been proven to work. But momentum can be lazy, complacent, and naïvely oblivious to market shifts that can pull the rug out from under it.

Clearly, you need both change and momentum to successfully grow your practice. You need change to secure your future and best position your resources to go after opportunities. You need momentum to give you time to build on successes and develop the infrastructure that allows you to scale. The two often come into conflict and cause tensions in a company.

How do you maintain this dynamic balance? While there is no perfect, permanent answer to this question, we do have a working solution that has produced amazing results for our businesses, and for tens of thousands of business owners with whom we've shared it. Once a year (we suggest December or early January), go off-site with your key team leaders and team members for a one-day strategic-planning retreat. Your assignment is to take a critical look at your long-term plan and examine the state of your practice with the following questions: What are the current market conditions? What trends are coming our way? Are our key objectives still the right ones? Is our strategy to get us there still working? Once you know the state of your practice and market, make any necessary big-picture corrections.

Then, every quarter, we recommend taking your key staff off-site for a half-day session to revisit this plan and concretely map out the next ninety days. You'll lay out your top three strategic priorities for the coming quarter, and write up a simple one-page Action Plan specifying exactly what you must do that quarter to grow and develop your practice. At the end of the quarter, you'll repeat the process. At the end of the year, you'll step back and do a fresh pass on your big-picture, long-term plan for your company.

The reason why this process works so well is because it prompts you to step out of the daily practice of medicine to look freshly at your practice every quarter, while also allowing your team to dive deep into the execution of your ninety-day Action Plan, which itself focuses on areas of maximal importance to your practice.

Without this clear framework, too many practice owners change their focus so often that their teams are left dizzy, feeling the vertigo of too much change, and frustrated because, just when they seem to be on the verge of really getting something big done, the owner has shifted the playing field yet again, forcing them to abandon projects prior to completion and wasting hours of their effort.

Done well, these quarterly ninety-day sprints reward your practice with the benefit of regular opportunities to change and adapt. But you also get the results that come from having momentum and disciplined execution on known priorities quarter by quarter.

In this chapter we'll dive deeper into this strategic structure that helps your practice effectively plan its path forward as you scale. This structure includes your annual planning and goal setting, and your map for the coming year. It also includes quarterly Action Planning, checkpoints to evaluate progress and gain clarity on upcoming goals, and weekly execution and accountability for getting the results you want.

Start with Annual Planning

This process begins by looking at the year ahead and asking the highest-level strategic questions. These questions include:

- **What practice are you trying to build?** Too many doctors never stop to clarify in writing what it is that they're working so hard to create.

- **What does your ideal practice look like quantitatively?** For example, how many patients do you want to serve? What annual profits do you want to achieve? What are other key numbers that describe the practice that you hope to build?

- **What does your ideal practice look like qualitatively?** For example, what is your reputation in the local medical community? In what types of procedures do you specialize? What do your patients say about you?

- **What is your personal role in that ideal practice?** For example, how many hours a week do you work? What are your responsibilities? What does your schedule look like? How many weeks of real vacation time do you take each year? What do you no longer have to deal with in the practice but now let other talented team members handle instead?

- **Where do you currently stand in relation to your top goal?** In other words, what's the gap? If you want to build a $10-million-per-year practice, how far from that goal are you today? Essentially, the job of strategic planning is to narrow that gap on a quarter-by-quarter basis.

Next, Find Your "Sweet Spot"

What is currently your practice's single biggest constraint to growth? What is the one ingredient that, if you had more of it, would allow your practice to grow most effectively?

While every practice has multiple limiting factors, each has one Limiting Factor (capital "L," capital "F") that does the most to constrain its growth in the here and now. Pushing back your biggest Limiting Factor is a major leverage point to growing your practice. One key way to grow your practice is to identify and push back your current Limiting Factor quarter by quarter. In the context of creating a true Level Three practice, you'll need to build the systems, team, controls, and culture to help you push back your Limiting Factor in the long term.

The more precisely you can identify your Limiting Factor, the easier it is to effectively push it back. For example, if you say your Limiting Factor is cash flow, you might come up with a dozen ideas to improve your cash flow, but many of them may be counterproductive because your initial diagnosis of your Limiting Factor is too broad. Is it a cash-flow challenge caused by low patient volume relative to your current clinical staffing and capacity? Or is it low cash flow caused by a poor mix of patient base and insurance payers? Is it an issue with your collections? Or, instead, is the real root cause of your cash-flow issue that your providers regularly don't follow the right procedures and best practices when they fill out the EMR system and miscode their clinical work, substantially lowering your earned reimbursements? As you can see, before you rush off to "solve" your Limiting Factor, you've got to carefully and accurately nail down your diagnosis in the first place.

Once you have a clear diagnosis of your Limiting Factor in hand, it's time to select the highest-leverage tactics to push back this Limiting Factor. We developed the three-part Sweet Spot Analysis Tool to help you do just that.

First, brainstorm a list of all the potential ideas you have to push back your Limiting Factor. Don't settle for five or six ideas. Push yourself to come up with at least ten ideas—or, ideally, fifteen to twenty. For example, if your Limiting Factor is a cash-flow challenge caused by low patient volume relative to your current staffing level and clinical capacity, your list of ideas could include: implementing a "friends and family" referral program, or past-patient reactivation strategies, which you'll read about in Chapter 8. Or you could begin to give community talks, or increase your online advertising budget, or reduce your staffing level, or . . . You get the idea. The key is to push yourself to come up with as many ideas as you can that could potentially help you push back your Limiting Factor. The best way to come up with a few great ideas is to first come up with a list of a **lot** of potential ideas.

Next, run your brainstormed list of potential tactics through two filters: what we call the "Low-Hanging Fruit" filter and the "Home Run" filter. "Low-Hanging Fruit" refers to a no-brainer opportunity that you're almost certain will be successful. While it may or may not have a big impact, it is fairly straightforward to implement and you have a very high level of confidence that it's going to work. A "Home Run," on the other hand, is an opportunity that, if all goes just right, will have a huge payoff for your business.

Go through each brainstormed idea on the list and ask, is this tactic a Low-Hanging Fruit? If it is, check the box in the "LH" column identifying it as a Low-Hanging Fruit.

Then, in a second, separate pass, go through your list of brainstormed ideas and ask of each item in turn, is this tactic a Home Run? If it is, check the box in the "HR" column.

What you're looking for are any tactics that are both Low-Hanging Fruit and Home Runs. These are what we call your "Sweet Spot" ideas: the highest-leverage choices to push back your Limiting Factor. Low-Hanging Fruit are easy to implement with high odds of success, and Home Runs offer big impact if they work. Your Sweet Spots are the first and best places to focus your practice's resources.

Finally, now that you've identified your Sweet Spot tactics, turn them into a mini Action Plan of who needs to do what by when. See Figure 3.1 for a sample Sweet Spot Analysis Tool. You can download a blank version of this tool as part of the free Practice Growth Tool Kit you receive along with this book. Just visit **www.GrowMyMedicalPractice.com**.

Now, Map Out Your Year—and Your Quarter

It's time to map out your year, and to do so by taking into consideration the important work you just did. In the next year, what progress do you want to make toward your most important three- to five-year goal? What is your revenue goal for the coming year? Your profit target? Any other key performance indicator (KPI) goals that, if you hit them, will increase your odds of making meaningful progress toward your one-year and three- to five-year goals? What is your strategy to reach these goals? (Hint: Use your Sweet Spot insights.)

Armed with this map of what you want to accomplish in the coming year, your next move is to create your quarterly Action Plan. Why quarterly? Because the quarter is the perfect unit of time to bridge your big-picture goals and your weekly planning and daily actions. It's long enough that you can get meaningful work done to bring you closer to your long-term goals, but short enough that you can hold your focus and frequently course-correct.

Here's the key: You're now going to outline your quarterly Action Plan *on a single page.* For more than a decade, we've pushed our coaching clients to follow a one-page Action Plan. Why one page, instead of two or twenty-five? Because we've learned from our work in coaching hundreds of doctors that, in the rush of the day-to-day, if your plan is two or three pages (or more), you just won't use it on a weekly basis to guide your execution. With a one-page plan, you can pin it above your desk and review

Sweet Spot Analysis™ Tool

Low-Hanging Fruit: Solution that would be easy to implement with a high chance of success.

Home Run: Solution that, if it worked, would have a BIG impact.

Sweet Spot: Solutions that are both Low-Hanging Fruit AND Home Runs.

LOW-HANGING FRUIT

SWEET SPOT

HOME RUN

Our single biggest Limiting Factor is...

Low patient volume relative to our current staffing level and fixed overhead

---

What are 10+ ideas to push this Limiting Factor back?

		LH	HR
1.	Friends and Family Referral Program.	☑	☑
2.	Past-patient reactivation strategy.	☑	☐
3.	Outreach system to physician community.	☐	☐
4.	Attend local medical community events to network.	☑	☐
5.	Hire a physician liaison to scale up referrals.	☐	☑
6.	Hire an online marketing company.	☐	☑
7.	Give community talks.	☐	☐
8.	Upgrade our website for SEO and lead capture.	☐	☐
9.	Cross market services between our 2 clinics.	☐	☐
10.	Direct mail to local community.	☐	☐
11.	Sponsor local charities and events.	☑	☐
12.	Determine our current best 2 lead generation tactics and invest more time/money to scale them.	☑	☑

Mini Action Plan

	Who	By When
Solution 1: Friends and Family Referral Program		
☐ Design offer.	Tim	1/21/xx
☐ Create collateral and train staff.	Tim	2/1/xx
☐ Launch and track weekly.	Tim	3/1/xx
☐ Formal check in—refine.	Tim	3/30/xx
☐		
Solution 2: Scale our best 2 tactics		
☐ Analyze past data—identify 2 best tactics.	Lee	1/31/xx
☐ Create mini-plan to scale.	Lee	2/15/xx
☐ Formal check in—refine.	Lee	2/28/xx
☐		
Solution 3: _____		
☐		
☐		
☐		
☐		
☐		

Copyright © Maui Mastermind®

Figure 3.1: The Sweet Spot Analysis Tool

it every week to pull the next action steps into your weekly task list. (You'll also be able to easily review key staff members' quarterly one-page Action Plans, and hold them accountable on a weekly basis.) In essence, your one-page Action Plan becomes your quarterly and weekly GPS to make sure that your team is focusing on the right things and hitting the key milestones on time.

See the sample Action Plan in Figure 3.2. To download a free template to create your practice's one-page Action Plan, just go to **www.GrowMyMedicalPractice.com**.

A Simple Three-Step Process to Create Your One-Page Practice Action Plan

Step One: Pick Your Top Three Focus Areas for the Quarter

Your top three Focus Areas represent the most important work of the coming quarter. Sure, you'll still need to tend to the day-to-day needs of your practice, but your Focus Areas are those that you've identified for investing a portion of your best resources—because you know these specific things will really help you scale.

Potential Focus Areas

- Improve billing collections

- Increase clinical capacity

- Increase patient volume

- Recruit another provider

- Conduct a margin analysis by procedure type or payer category

- Hire a director of operations

- Mitigate a key practice legal exposure

- Negotiate a new contract with the hospital

- Find a location to build our surgical center

Don't go overboard! We strongly advise that you limit yourself to three Focus Areas as your top priorities for each quarter. Why? Because ninety

Quarterly Action Plan for: Q1, 20XX

Focus Area One:
Increase patient volume

Action Steps/Milestones	Who	By When
❏ Lay out current system and tracking to see what historic performance reveals. Use insights in next action step to pick tactics to increase patient volume.	John	1/15/XX
❏ Conduct "Sweet Spot" analysis and choose the top 2 marketing ideas to implement in Q1. Rough out plan to implement and systemize each.	John	1/31/XX
❏ Create a draft "Marketing Scorecard" to use to track daily patient sources.	John	1/31/XX
❏ Checkpoint 1: How is KPI going? Review how implementation of 2 new tactics going. What is working well? What simple tweaks should we make?	John	2/28/XX
❏ Review status at end of quarter and then refine next steps for Q2 based on where we stand.	John	3/21/XX

Criteria of Success:

• Have solid scorecard in place tracking patient sources.

• Increase patient volume by 15% over quarter.

KPI: # of patient visits/day per provider

Focus Area Two:
Begin to systemize the front desk role of our practice

Action Steps/Milestones	Who	By When
❏ Brainstorm all the "front desk" systems we think we'll eventually want from scheduling patients, handling phone and email, patient check-in, etc.	Sarah	1/15/XX
❏ Have system one completed and team trained on its use.	Sarah	2/7/XX
❏ Checkpoint: How is system working? What is going well? What refinements need to be made? What training adjustments are needed? Lay out key action steps.	Sarah	2/28/XX
❏ Have 2nd system built and team trained to use. (Checkpoint to review and refine in early Q2.)	Sarah	3/15/XX
❏ Review list of "sales associate" systems needed. Decide on the next 2–3 most important systems to build and implement. Rough out a plan to do this for Q2.	Sarah	3/30/XX

Criteria of Success:

• Have an outline of the front desk role (we'll flesh out these systems over Q2 and Q3).

• Have chosen and built out version 1.0 of the most important front desk systems.

KPI: % Completed (estimate)

Focus Area Three:
Hiring process for new nursing staff member

Action Steps/Milestones	Who	By When
❏ Create draft of job description and help wanted ad. Review both with Pam. Revise based on her input.	Sarah	2/15/XX
❏ Create draft of interview process, key questions to ask, and the 3–5 "must-have" qualifications of hire. Review draft with Pam and revise based on her input.	Sarah	3/7/XX
❏ Create draft outline of new hire orientation process. Review with Pam and revise based on her input.	Sarah	3/21/XX
❏ Create 1–2 page "new hire checklist" of above steps from job ad posting through hire and first 30 days of orientation.	Sarah	3/30/XX

Criteria of Success:

• Have a written job description and help wanted ad.

• Written outline of interview process and key questions and qualifications.

• Written outline of a "new hire" orientation process to follow.

Copyright © Maui Mastermind®

Figure 3.2: Sample Action Plan

days pass quickly, and if you spread your practice too thin, you'll find yourself partially doing a bunch of things instead of fully attending to a few key items that actually produce value. Less is often more when it comes to executing on your ninety-day Action Plan.

Step Two: Determine Success Criteria for Your Focus Areas

Now that you've picked your three Focus Areas for the quarter, the temptation is to immediately determine your action steps. Don't. Instead, pause and clarify your criteria of success within each Focus Area. What would you need to accomplish this quarter in this Focus Area to be successful? What can you actually *observe and measure* that will signal your success? This gives you a clear yardstick against which to gauge progress, and paints a clear picture of what success in this Focus Area, this quarter, looks like.

In order to limit your Action Plan to one page, pick three or four definite criteria of success for each Focus Area, including one key performance indicator (KPI) that you'll track. Now that you've got your written criteria of success in hand, step three will be easy. Go back and review the sample Action Plan in Figure 3.2.

Step Three: Lay Out Key Action Steps and Milestones for the Quarter

The final step is to determine the key actions and milestones that are necessary to meet your criteria of success for each Focus Area over the coming quarter. Break each Focus Area down into between five and seven action steps and milestones. While your plan should be detailed enough to guide your actions, it shouldn't be so detailed that you feel overwhelmed or lose yourself in minutiae.

For each action step, pick a specific team member to be ultimately responsible for executing that step by a specific date. While you can have multiple people contribute to a specific step or steps, you need to pick one person who is tasked with the responsibility and authority to get that step done and done well. This person will "own" the task. This designation of ownership will be critical to your success. It's hard to hold anyone accountable for missed milestones when it wasn't clear who was really responsible in the first place.

With this structure, the owner of any given task doesn't have to do all of the work herself; she just needs to be responsible for making sure that it gets done in the best way possible. Over time, as you become fluent in this planning process, you'll have each of your key people create their own department's one-page quarterly Action Plan. Their Action Plan is the link between their department's targets and the most important priorities of the practice as a whole.

The final element of your strategic structure is your weekly accountability. While we recommend the quarter as the unit to connect your big-picture goals and objectives to the practical level of execution, we recommend that you use the week as your basic unit to connect execution of your strategic plan to your in-the-trenches work, day in and day out.

The Big Rock Report

We've developed what we call the "Big Rock Report" to help you in your weekly execution of tasks. At the start of each week, you and your key staff members will review your quarterly Action Plan. Next, each of you will pick two or three "Big Rocks." Big Rocks are specific action steps, tasks, or chunks of a key project that, if you did them in the coming week, would do the most to help you accomplish the key results outlined in your quarterly Action Plan. Why do we call them "Big Rocks"? Because it's with these actions that you build your success, week by week, quarter by quarter, year by year.

Each Big Rock should be something that takes no more than two hours. If it's likely to take longer, then break it down into smaller chunks. Why two hours or less? Because, even following the time-mastery strategies you learned in the last chapter, it's unlikely that you'll consistently be able to block out a bigger chunk of time in your schedule. By limiting your Big Rocks to steps that you can complete in a one- to two-hour time frame, you'll increase your odds of getting them done.

The first part of your weekly "Big Rock Report" is to review how you did on your prior week's Big Rocks. Did you get them all done? What were the outcomes? What next steps are needed? What other information do you want to share with your team on this item?

The report then lists key victories, challenges, and other updates (see Figure 3.3). Finally, the Big Rock Report ends with you and your key team members reviewing your one-page Action Plan to pick your Big Rocks for the coming week. What steps do you need to take this week to keep yourself on target to meet or exceed your quarterly plan?

The way this works with David's business-coaching clients is that they get their key team members to fill out this report through a simple web-based app each week. This gives you, the practice owner, a simple one-page view of each person's focus and results each week. You can use this report to celebrate victories, troubleshoot challenges, and, when needed,

Weekly Big Rock Report - Period Ending March 19th, 20XX

Last Week's Big Rocks

Big Rocks	Comments
☑ 1) Complete draft of updated marketing scoreboard.	• Finished the draft. Created version in Excel too. • Still need to build in automated formulas for "month-to-date," "quarter-to-date," and "year-to-date" views of marketing results. Will ask Andrea to do those formulas next week. • Have past data in the scoreboard from start of year. Will be updating weekly and emailing out monthly going forward.
☑ 2) Do final version of "Clinic Nurse" job description and recruitment ad.	• Ad was placed via MGMA website and two online sites. • So far we've had 12 candidates and counting. I'll report more on this next week.

Business Review

Key Victories

Have a working scoreboard for marketing for first time which shows all sources for new patients.

Staff covered really well for three clinical teams at Vanderway Clinic who were out sick last week.

Key Business Challenges

Lots of illness in management and staff, making staffing and scheduling tougher.

Key Updates

Looks to have found strong candidate for PA for Vanderway Clinic (will make offer next week).

Carlotta Clinic staff reviews completed.

Placing ad for nursing staff member for Vanderway Clinic this coming week.

Next Week's Big Rocks

Big Rocks	Comments
1) Hiring steps (resume reviews, first round phone interviews) for key Clinic Nurse for Vanderway.	
2) Get Andrea to put formulas into marketing scoreboard Excel so we see trends/bigger picture of patient sources MTD, QTD, YTD.	

Copyright © Maui Mastermind®

Figure 3.3: The Big Rock Report

to redirect staff efforts to better and higher uses. Done right, it only takes your key team members five to ten minutes each week to fill out, and it takes you only a few minutes to read. It's a powerful tool to help you grow your business and get your life back.

Now that you've crafted your practice's strategic Action Plan, you're on your way to the kind of success that Dr. Hamil, Dr. Padda, and Dr. Lara have achieved. Remember, they used the same strategies that you're using—and you can enjoy the same results.

And as you move closer toward your goal of having a scalable, Level Three owner-independent practice, you will also need to do some important work on how the work gets done. That is, your practice will need to have great systems in place before you can bring it to scale and finally reclaim the personal time that you need and deserve. The next chapter has you covered.

4

Step Four: Build Your Master System

D
r. Challa is a very successful gastroenterologist and the founder of the Kansas Medical Clinic, a large and growing medical practice with offices across Kansas. As his practice expanded, however, Dr. Challa and his team began to experience the challenges of outgrowing the systems that had worked so well when they were a single-location GI clinic with close oversight from Dr. Challa.

Remember that old PBS television show called *This Old House*? Imagine you're on it, working on a seventy-five-year-old house with its original electrical wiring and plumbing. What would happen if you plugged in to that house a full complement of modern electrical appliances? You'd blow your fuses, not to mention risk an electrical fire. And what would happen to your plumbing if you went from a well-water system to tapping into the higher pressure of city water? (Can you say "rain gear"?)

The same is true for the systems you use to scale your medical practice. Too much growth that places increasing demands on old, outdated systems can put the whole operation under water. The systems that worked for a $2.5-million-a-year, single-office practice are no longer sufficient to cope with a $15-million, five-location practice, and not even close to being adequate for a $53-million-a-year multicity practice. At first, the additional sales will cause a few "leaks," but before long, your practice will have burst pipes and water everywhere.

Of course the first major hurdle most practices face in efficiently and consistently running the various functional "pillars" of their practice (i.e., marketing, clinical, HR, finance, etc.) is that they don't have formal business systems. Instead, they lean heavily on the individual ability and informal systems that a few key office team members hold in their head (or perhaps on sticky notes around their desk). What happens if one of these team members gets hurt? Of if her spouse gets transferred and she puts in her notice? Just like you want to protect your practice and all of your employees should anything happen to you, you need to protect your practice in case a proverbial "bus" hits one of your key employees.

Your business systems are a crucial stabilizing factor to protect the practice, your staff, and your patients (not to mention all of their respective families, who indirectly rely upon the practice). So, just what *are* systems?

Systems are reliable processes and procedures that empower your practice to efficiently and consistently operate to profitably produce great health services for your patients. They're documented best practices that increase your practice's efficiency and reduce costly mistakes. Systems include documents and processes, such as the checklists your clinical team follows to ensure that patients get the optimal health outcome, as well as the orientation process you put all new hires through, the standardized contracts you use with your vendors, and even the scripts your phone team uses to convert phone inquiries into new patients. Your business systems include any company know-how of how to run and operate your medical practice that is captured in a tangible format versus locked in the brain of an individual team member.

Let's return to Dr. Challa. When he first began working with David's coaching team several years ago, one of the most impactful outcomes of the program for his practice was introducing and institutionalizing the creation, organization, use, and refinement of formal systems across the practice. Up until that point Dr. Challa's team had had a hodgepodge of business systems. If one of his clinics had a particularly skilled clinic director, that location developed powerful tools (i.e., systems) to help it operate smoothly and effectively. But thirty miles away, at a different location, those best practices might very well be totally unknown.

Think of how much Dr. Challa's practice invested—in terms of staff time and attention—to create those systems at the first clinic. Yet those practices remained entirely siloed, unavailable to their team members down the road. Further, as the practice grew still larger, it needed its systems to grow with it, but there was no formal culture inside the practice of creating, using, refining, and *sharing* best practices across locations.

The challenge wasn't just a matter of formalizing best practices in writing, either. Dr. Challa's team was consistently frustrated and wasting time on things as simple as trying to find a vendor contract because there was no central, organized storage location for all their developed systems. This lack of a structure to house and access their systems wasted time and hindered the efficiency and growth of the practice. "Somebody gives an important file a name and puts it in a folder," Dr. Challa told us, "while someone else goes looking for it, can't find it fast enough, and ends up creating another file."

This happened in lots of different situations. When his staff began interviewing to hire a new physician, they drafted a term sheet to summarize salary, benefits, bonuses, and terms of employment. They ended up conducting three interviews in a six-month period—but every time they needed that document, they couldn't find where they had put it. They recreated that term sheet three times!

This isn't a sexy problem, but it's exceedingly common—and costly. And even as the Kansas Medical Clinic was outwardly successful, and increasingly in demand among patients in their region, Dr. Challa knew they needed to solve this internal problem if they wanted to continue to grow their regional medical group to more locations.

In this chapter, you're going to learn a powerful concept called your "UBS," which stands for "Ultimate Business System." It was a concept that David created close to two decades ago, when he was scaling one of his large companies. Your UBS is both the organized collection of systems you develop and use to run your clinic, as well as the term that reminds your team to make the daily use, storage, refinement, and sharing of systems a part of the culture of your practice.

Most commonly, your UBS is an organized collection of digital folders of practice systems that are stored in the cloud. Your practice systems can include things like the following:

- Checklists for new-patient paperwork, clinical procedures, and even the cleaning of an exam room
- Standardized paperwork for new hires, HIPAA releases, and post-procedure release documentation
- Databases of key information on referring medical groups, reimbursement-coding "cheat sheets," and vendor pricing
- Documented processes and step-by-step instructions on how to use your EMR system, collect and process co-pays at patient checkout, and send out your monthly patient e-letter
- FAQs for new patients as well as common Q&A documents and instructions for staff on how to handle common situations, how to create more consistent service results from your vendors, and any number of other topics

Think of your UBS as the doorway through which to introduce systems thinking across your team. This UBS tool will also give you a coherent and scalable way to store the systems your team creates, so that your entire team—even if members are spread across multiple locations, like Dr. Challa's—will be able to instantly access your systems from wherever they are.

"It took us four months to build our UBS," said Dr. Challa. "Whether it's fee schedules, invoicing, vendor contracts, HR materials, or step-by-step processes for how we do our work, it's all itemized in the UBS. It's been a lifesaver. Now, when I want a document, it's on my desk within three minutes."

That efficiency was a great help to Dr. Challa as he built the Kansas Medical Clinic into what it is today: a practice that spans four specialties and has nine locations with 120 employees spread over a hundred-mile area. "Put it in the UBS" has become a company mantra.

And it's not just Dr. Challa. By implementing a UBS at *your* practice, you'll change the way work gets done. Now it's time to get into the mechanics of how your practice will build and leverage its own UBS.

Replace Chaos with Stability and Scalability

If your practice lacks a UBS, you generally have a random collection of files spread across a dozen different team members' computers, or worse, stored informally in their heads. When your office manager finally comes up with a better, wrinkle-free process for onboarding new patients, that process will live in her head and nowhere else—unless you have a UBS where she can record and file it. When an administrator determines an effective strategy for dealing with a particular insurer, he may jot down some reminders on a sticky note—but if he leaves the practice, that knowledge will leave with him. Unless you have a UBS.

To be clear, your UBS is not a policies and procedures manual (which few employees will ever use!). Your UBS is an organized collection of tools in one central location that captures the actual everyday know-how of your practice in a searchable, accessible, and editable way. It's stored inside a simple hierarchy of digital file folders, generally in a cloud-based system, and includes things like your checklists, spreadsheets, proposal templates, training videos, and sample marketing pieces. Your UBS is the master system for how your practice structures, organizes, stores, accesses, and refines its internal knowledge. It's a way to gather all of that information in one place and give your whole team access to it.

As you move toward the goal of building an owner-independent practice, your UBS will be a key ingredient in making that possible. Your UBS is a means of implementing controls in the daily work of your practice—not *control* in the sense that you or another manager will oversee every little thing, but *controls*—plural—in that reliable procedures will govern your team's daily work.

Few people enjoy being micromanaged, so the UBS plays the important role of making key information easily accessible, and therefore turning the *default* behavior into the *right* behavior. The more your controls help individual team members make decisions on a daily basis, the more smoothly and efficiently your practice will run, regardless of whether or not you're physically present. When you empower your team with strong systems that give structure to a process or responsibility, and train your staff on how to use those systems, you're setting your team up to *win*.

Based on David's work with thousands of businesses across North America, what's clear is that systems are not a matter of "one conversation, and you're done." Instead, they must be an ongoing, living theme that you champion in your practice, not only until you get genuine buy-in from your staff, but until your staff members *internalize* how to create, use, refine, and share these best practices as a normal part of their office day.

As Dr. Challa's example illustrates, the UBS is a way of starting this important dialogue at your practice. You'll know you've won when you regularly hear team members say, "Did you add that to the UBS?" and "Great solution! Can you UBS it?"

A Simple Four-Step Process to Build Your UBS

Following is a simple four-step process to begin constructing your UBS over the next ninety days.

Step One: Create your UBS's file folder organizational hierarchy.

If you had to cluster all the functions of your practice into between five and nine primary areas, which we'll call "pillars," what would they be?

Most medical groups will use the following six pillars to organize their UBS:

1.0 Marketing

2.0 HR

3.0 Clinical

4.0 Leadership

5.0 Administrative/Operations

6.0 Financial

Step Two: Pick one area, and break it into between five and seven subareas.

Now you'll break each area into its subareas (see Figure 4.1). Let's say you start with HR. In that case, your subareas might look like this:

2.0 HR

2.1 Recruitment and Hiring

2.2 Onboarding and Orientation

2.3 Training

2.4 Benefits and HR Admin

2.5 Exiting

Step Three: Populate this area and its subareas with existing systems.

Look through each of your team's hard drives and see what systems you already have. Ask the appropriate members of your team to look through their work area for the tools, documents, and informal systems they are individually using in this area of your practice that you may want to formally add to your UBS. You'll be surprised by how many documents and materials are known to only one person. And you'll be horrified to realize how many out-of-date files your staff members are still using because they didn't know that an updated version was available somewhere else. As you go through your team's computers, purge outdated materials, identify which items are inadequate and need updating, determine which materials work well, and decide which items you will need to create from scratch.

Save to your UBS only those documents and tools that you want your practice to use going forward. (You can store any outdated items in an "archive" folder in each section of your UBS, on the off chance that you'll need it later.)

Key Point: Rename every file you put into your UBS so it's obvious and easy to search for later. Think keywords. Don't name a file based on what the person who created it thinks it should be called; name it in terms of what someone else is most likely to search for. *Standardize* your key

Your "UBS": The System of All Your Systems

1.0 Marketing
1.1 Lead Generation
1.2 Lead Conversion
1.3 Planning and Strategy
1.4 Branding

2.0 HR
2.1 Hiring/Onboarding
2.2 Training/Review/Retention
2.3 Compliance
2.4 Outsourcing
2.5 Exit Processes

3.0 Clinical
3.1 EMR System
3.2 Patient Care & Flow
3.3 Providers
3.4 Support Functions

4.0 Leadership
4.1 Strategic Planning
4.2 Leadership Devlp/Continuity
4.3 Company Culture
4.4 Communication

5.0 Admin/Ops
5.1 General Administration
5.2 Facilities
5.3 Ops
5.4 Purchasing

6.0 Financial
6.1 Accounting/Reporting
6.2 A/R (Collections)
6.3 A/P (Payables)
6.4 Budgeting and Planning
6.5 Financial Controls
6.6 Cash Flow Management

Your "UBS" is your "Ultimate Business System." It is your master system for how you organize, store, access, and refine your systems. Your goal is to make your UBS a living breathing way of doing business in your company. You'll know you've won when you regularly hear your team say things like, *"Did you add that to the UBS?"* and *"Great solution to that problem, can you UBS it?"* This is not something you'll do in one sitting, but rather it is a way of approaching your business that you'll engage your entire team in owning over the long term.

Copyright © Maui Mastermind®

Figure 4.1: Your Master System

naming conventions. For example, if one of Dr. Challa's staff members called the term sheet for an offer to a new provider the "provider offer form" and the next person went to search for it as the "term sheet for new physician," they wouldn't find it. And, not finding it, they would likely recreate it. Not only would this be an obvious waste of time, but what if this new term sheet wasn't as good as the previous version? Or, what if it was better, but the next time the initial staff member went to search for the "provider offer form" she pulled up her old version, forgoing the benefit of the better version that the second staff member had created? You get the point. What's more, as your staff is increasingly drawn from the digital generation—for which search has become the common default for finding facts—if they can't find what they're looking for within two minutes, they'll assume it doesn't exist and build it from scratch.

From now on, team members will look for a tool by searching in your UBS. If they don't quickly and easily find what they want, then they'll give up and either re-create it or wing it. By naming files to make them intuitive and easy to find, not only will the team use the right tool, but also, your systems will get the benefit of any refinement that your team members add as they go about their daily work.

Step Four: Pick one or two systems to build this quarter for this area.

Ask yourself, "If we could build one or two systems in this area of the practice in the next ninety days, which would be most valuable?" For example, if you really need a good onboarding system for your CNAs, then start building out your system in that area. The key is to start with one area of your UBS and build from there. It will get easier as you go. Remember, it took Dr. Challa's team four months to create their initial UBS—and they've been enhancing it and reaping the benefits ever since.

Each Quarter, Repeat Steps Two to Four

Over time, this process is magic. You'll find that you're making your practice less reliant on the private knowledge of a few key staff members (including, and especially, *your* knowledge), and that, in turn, is making the practice more scalable and putting it squarely on the path to owner independence.

Remember that the UBS will not work if it's just a fad at your office. If you start the process and don't see it through, your efforts will wither and you'll lose credibility with your team. The UBS has to become the ingrained way of doing things at your practice.

Enlist Key Team Members in Building Your UBS

There are several reasons why you should not build your practice's UBS by yourself. For one thing, we're trying to reduce your workload, not add to it. But even more important, it's crucial that you get team buy-in. The systems contained in the UBS are primarily for your staff, so team members should be integral in designing them. In just the way that you enlisted staff to take ownership of key items in your Action Plan, you'll do the same here. And as you involve your team in this process, you'll have the opportunity to talk with them about the value of the systems you're creating together. Point out that everyone's job will be easier and everyone will enjoy more autonomy when the UBS is in place. Share your commitment to becoming a systems-driven culture, and ask for their help in taking key steps to move toward that goal.

"I'd like us to work toward our stated goal of turning this practice into one that's more stable and less reliant on me personally," you might say to your practice manager or lead nurse. "You're a key player. Would you be willing to help by writing up a system to ensure that we're entering patient records correctly?"

Now she owns that task. At a predetermined point in the future, the two of you will meet to check in on progress. She will become a champion of the UBS, and suddenly you'll have multiple voices pushing it forward and using it to guide employee behavior. Ultimately, you want your whole team to see why systems and controls make a difference for all of you.

Where to Store Your UBS

Every company needs to come up with a means of storing its systems for the whole team to use. Technologies change, but at its core, your UBS will always require a storage method that has the following four attributes:

1. **Accessibility:** It needs to be quickly accessible. Usually, this means it's cloud based.

2. **Searchability:** It needs to be easily searchable. People have to be able to quickly find what they want, or they'll start keeping their own systems at their desks or on their computers. Eventually this would mean your UBS wouldn't house the most up-to-date practices, and that would defeat its purpose.

3. **Version Control:** It needs to be collaborative, which means all users need to be able to edit and improve the data. This requires version control. It also means the UBS should be constantly pruned of outdated information. Systems will change and grow, and if you leave old items to live with the new, they'll make it harder for people to quickly determine which systems to use and when.

4. **Security:** It needs to have secure features that allow you to protect your intellectual property both from outside parties and from internal misuse. Even though you'll be keeping your patient records primarily in your EMR system, we strongly suggest that you pick a storage solution for your UBS that is HIPAA compliant.

Because technology is changing so fast, we've listed on our website our current best suggestions for a hosted solution to house your UBS. To view them, please visit **www.GrowMyMedicalPractice.com**.

It's a Dimmer, Not a Light Switch

You're not going to be able to design, create, and implement your UBS in one fell swoop. And in fact, you shouldn't. It takes time to get team buy-in and develop systems that people will actually use. Rather than thinking of the UBS as a light switch that you can just flick to the "on" position, think of it as a dimmer knob that you'll turn to steadily brighten the lights. The UBS will come alive bit by bit, over time. That's how it will become a part of your culture, the norm for how you and your team execute the core work of your practice. Dr. Challa did it—and so can you.

Now take a moment to congratulate yourself. You're on your way to making powerful changes to the way you manage your time, determine your core work and goals, and execute that core work on a daily basis at your practice. These are huge steps on the path to building a practice that's owner independent.

And now that you've taken these important steps, it's time to accelerate.

PART TWO

APPLY THE SIX PRACTICE ACCELERATORS TO GO FASTER

CHAPTER 5

Accelerator One: Strengthen Your Core

In Part One of this book, you learned the foundation of building an owner-independent practice. You've learned essential time-management strategies to help you quit doing low-value activities and focus your energies on the highest-value work. You've become familiar with key tactics for making strategic choices, with your one-page Action Plan now serving as the map for your team's daily, weekly, and quarterly work.

You also now have a blueprint in hand for constructing and implementing your Ultimate Business System, through which your team members will make sharing best practices and systematizing key processes a consistent part of their routine work, thereby reducing reliance on any one individual and maturing your practice into an efficient, scalable enterprise. Now it's time to build on that foundation to grow and mature your practice even faster.

In Part Two of this book, you're going to learn about the six practice accelerators.

We'll start by focusing on strengthening your core—how your practice and team produce your actual medical services. In a moment, we'll share with you a simple four-step process to begin this work on the delivery of your core services, but first, we want to share a story with you.

In 2001, Dr. Singh founded Access Health Care. His vision for his fledgling new practice was to enrich lives by providing a healing touch. When he began to expand Access, Dr. Singh knew that he wanted to build a practice that truly supported this core mission. He wanted to serve more and more patients in alignment with that vision. In practical terms, this meant building a coordinated front- and back-office team of people who were entirely dedicated to empowering and enabling providers to see more patients and to provide a consistently high level of care.

There was a time when Dr. Singh was accustomed to seeing thirty patients a day. At the same time, though, he knew that he was capable of seeing forty-five patients a day. His goal wasn't to work harder, but to build the core systems and team that would allow him to see those forty-five patients in the same amount of time he used to see thirty, and to do so without compromising the quality of care—and indeed, while *increasing* quality. He knew it was possible.

But on the path toward that vision, Dr. Singh hit roadblocks. When he first began to talk with members of his team about scaling their practice and bringing their core vision to more patients, he found that not everyone was on board. One of his key administrators couldn't handle the new direction. Suddenly the work ahead of her required a different skill set, and it was a skill set that she lacked. This isn't uncommon, and it's just the sort of pain point that can keep a practice from accelerating its growth.

This administrator's unease became increasingly obvious. When Dr. Singh brought in a new staff member, the old administrator didn't want the new person to succeed, and acted accordingly. This could have sabotaged their growth and set them back half a year. Though he was grateful for this person's years of service, it became obvious that she could not remain in her role. When Dr. Singh brought in a new CFO to oversee the financial end of Access's growth, the embattled administrator got upset and resigned. This was a painful period, and yet it was necessary if the Access team was going to accomplish its vision of healing more and more people.

"It's possible to create the front- and back-office systems and teams where everyone is so focused on the vision of healing that they will continuously make your job easier," says Dr. Singh today. Though he didn't understand exactly how to do that when he started out in 2001, he has learned that every single staff member, from the back-office workers and case managers to mid-level physician extenders and employed physicians, all must play a coordinated role in running a better practice and supporting a shared vision.

It didn't happen overnight, but Dr. Singh eventually reached his goal of seeing 50 percent more patients each day. "Now, on my Push Days, I'm able to see forty-five patients, because I have the systems and staff in place to help me," he says. At the same time, his practice has achieved impressive quality scores across report cards from Freedom, Humana, Optimum, and others.

Interestingly enough, the administrator who had left his practice soon got a job at a nearby radiology office. Five years later, Access bought that radiology center. Once again, that administrator became Dr. Singh's employee—and once again, she was successful in her role, as she had been during her first years of employment. She is no longer responsible for tasks related to scaling the practice, but she's great at executing her specific job within the realm of radiology.

Dr. Singh wasn't always an expert at organizing his practice for growth and efficiency. On the contrary, he learned much of what he knows today as a result of painful and expensive trial and error as well as having watched other physicians' practices struggle or even fail. He didn't have this book, nor did he have the coaching resources that are available to you and your practice today.

And that's what this chapter is all about: giving you a simple methodology for strengthening the core of your practice.

Step One: Create Your Flowchart

What would it look like if you followed a patient walking around your office, mapping out their every sequential step as you welcomed, examined, treated, and checked them out? Map these steps into a simple flowchart—box to box to box—of all the steps they went through and experienced in the course of their interaction with your practice.

During a typical office visit, the patient checks in, waits in the waiting room, is brought in by a medical assistant, has vital signs checked, is brought to an exam room to be seen by a provider, and then proceeds to check out and exit. Depending on your type of practice and the types of procedures you perform, your patients may follow a similar path or it may be quite different. In either case, the first step to strengthening your core requires you to become clear on the visual steps of how your practice flows from the perspective of your patient. This will help you understand how to improve efficiency and productivity as well as patient satisfaction and quality of care.

Once you've laid that process out visually, do the same thing from the perspective of your most expensive providers: your physicians. While you can later look at your process through the eyes of your mid-level providers, nursing staff, and even office staff, for now, just focus on your most expensive and difficult-to-replace team members: your physician providers.

Follow them through the flow of what they do and where they go, step by step, as they treat patients and perform procedures. With this raw information in hand, it's time to move on to step two.

Step Two: Audit the Process

Gather together a small team of your key people in a conference room for ninety minutes to take a fresh look at the way you produce your core medical services. Put your two flowcharts up on the wall. Start with the patient-view flowchart, and ask the following questions:

- What jumps out at you as not making sense about this process? For example, is the waiting room simply dead time rather than a place where patients receive valuable education? Do you have doctors physically moving in a chaotic flow back and forth to both ends of your facility, and does this chaos eat up extra minutes of every day each week? Are physicians handling parts of the process that medical assistants could do instead?

- How could you reduce the number of steps in your overall process? For example, could you show educational videos in the waiting room so that nurses are not tasked with conveying the same educational material to every patient? Could you reduce wait times?

- How could you spend a little more money and get an exponential increase in production efficiency? For example, could you hire a medical tech to team up with each physician to speed up charting and note recording in your EMR system as each physician progresses from patient to patient? What about installing better Wi-Fi or upgrading your computers to speed up your providers' access of the EMR system itself?

- What frictions are there in the process that are bogging everything else down? How could you streamline your process to remove or at least minimize these factors? For instance, could you employ a scribe who accompanies a provider, so that provider can give full attention to the patient without typing into the EMR?

- What steps are missing that, if you added them to the process, would improve the efficiency, consistency, and/or quality of care for your patients? For example, could you create an enrichment center next to the waiting room so that patients can be educated, entertained, and/or engaged? Could you have medical assistants do preliminary screenings and then leave a note to bring the physician's attention to the reason for the visit?

■ What are your most expensive constraints to seeing more patients or performing more procedures? Is it your physical space? Or a lack of key providers? Or perhaps a lack of certain systems or automation? Identifying your most expensive constraints will give you clues about how to refine your core workflow to maximize around these constraints.

Now take a second pass at these questions, and this time, focus specifically on the physician's flow diagram. After thirty to forty-five minutes of brainstorming ideas with your key team members, move on to step three.

Step Three: Pick Your "Sweet Spot(s)" to Implement

Based on David's experiences in coaching practices through this process, at this point you've got an overwhelming mass of ideas that you know you "should" do to improve your core practice flow. But let's get real; there is simply no way you and your team can implement all these ideas at one time. In fact, doing so would be so disruptive to your current activities that your practice would actually suffer.

Instead, go back over your list of possible practice enhancements and flow fixes, and apply the "Low-Hanging Fruit" and "Home Run" filters you learned about in Chapter 3. Go through the full list and ask yourself, "Is this a Low-Hanging Fruit?" In other words, is this idea easy to put into practice, and are you fairly certain it will work? If it is, mark that idea with an "LH" for Low-Hanging Fruit.

Then, do a second, separate pass and ask of each item on your list, "Is this a Home Run?" In other words, if it works, will it have a BIG impact on the efficiency, consistency, or quality of the way you produce your medical services? If the answer is yes, mark that item with an "HR."

Now go back to your list and pull out all the items you've listed that are both Low-Hanging Fruit and Home Runs. These are your practice's core Sweet Spots. If you have a manageable number, which is rare, then you can jump to creating your execution mini plan.

Likely, though, you still have too many Sweet Spot ideas to execute over the next ninety days. That's great, since every Sweet Spot idea is, by definition, a high-leverage idea. As your starting point, pick one to three of them to implement over the next ninety days. Remember, start with less, but make sure that the less you start with matters more. By doing it this way, not only will you implement these fewer ideas better and faster, but you'll also be building your team's ability and motivation to bite off the next bunch of Sweet Spot ideas from this list next quarter, to continue the process of strengthening your practice's core.

Take your few Sweet Spot ideas and turn them into a mini game plan to execute on them. Who needs to do what by when? We encourage you to download the Sweet Spot Analysis Tool, which you can get for free at **www.GrowMyMedicalPractice.com**.

Step Four: Formalize Your Winners

After you've implemented your first few core process-improvement Sweet Spot ideas, observe which of the ideas you've tried have worked well. We call these your "winners." The strategic principle is to "Feed your winners; starve your losers." When you find a core process improvement that clearly works, formalize it. This means building a formal system for it and adding it to your UBS. It also means training all of your team on its use.

Essentially what this does is help your practice *institutionalize* the best of your workflow refinements. Now the key knowledge to run your practice isn't in the hands (or heads) of only one or two experienced team members, but, rather, it has been absorbed by the practice itself. Next quarter, repeat this process of picking your next round of Sweet Spot enhancements and formalize the ideas that have been proven to work.

Expand Your Capacity by Bringing on Another Provider

As you follow the structure and coaching we're sharing in this book, it's very likely that, at some point, no matter how efficient you make your core, you will run into a capacity challenge and need to bring on another provider. Whether you're a small solo-provider practice looking to bring on your first employed provider, or a large multi-clinic, multi-provider practice with numerous offices, or somewhere in between, at some point, strengthening your core will likely mean bringing on one or more providers.

But we're realistic. We know that it's hard to find and hire a physician who can give you the hours and flexibility you need. So we're not asking you to start there. Instead, start with the Low-Hanging Fruit of hiring a new mid-level provider.

If you think you can't afford to do that either, then take a second to consider Dr. Singh's experience. A few years into the start of his private practice, he kept running up against the problem of limited clinical capacity. He was desperate to hire another provider, though he was also certain that he couldn't afford it. He remembers it as a painful $80,000-a-year decision.

But rather than being held back by his fear of the risk, Dr. Singh took the leap. He brought in a new mid-level provider—a physician's assistant. Not only was the PA profitable for the practice, but also, she took some of the clinical load off his shoulders. Soon enough, he found that the presence of this PA on the team had freed up about 10 percent of his time. That may not sound like much, but getting 10 percent of your time back is a very big deal—especially if you use that newfound time for A- and B-level work, which is exactly what Dr. Singh did, investing that block of time in those activities that helped Access grow to the next level.

Every doctor who made that scary leap to bring on his or her first provider, whether it was a PA, or a medical tech to perform a specific

What I Do Best: Dr. Singh's Experience

I used to try to do everything, from the day-to-day management of my practice to fixing the Wi-Fi in our office (yes, really). These days, I'm clear about three things: what I do best, what I love best, and what gives me the best return. Everything else is unessential—I delegate it and let it go. I actually enjoy the management of the practice, but my management team is better at it than I am. So I let them do it.

Meanwhile, my job is strategic. It's figuring out our overall strategy and direction. That's my core, and it's my A Time. Of course, my time is most effective when everyone else is assisting me. That should be their goal. This isn't about ego; it's about getting the best results. My team members should be oriented toward helping me do what I do best—to the point that they should be selected and hired in such a way that that's their core.

onsite treatment, or even an employed physician, felt the fear and ambivalence about making that first key clinical hire. Yet, at some point, you cannot have an owner-independent medical practice if you are the only provider. You *need* other providers.

Dr. Singh couldn't have gotten to where he is today—with eighty-three distinct locations (yes, *eighty-three*), 1,003 employees, and hundreds of affiliate practices under the Access umbrella—if he hadn't taken the leap to hire that first provider when he thought he couldn't afford it.

Now, Upscale Your Practice

The final move to strengthen your core is to do what we call "upscaling" your practice. For a simple example of what it means to upscale, consider the time your patients spend in your waiting room. Are they being treated with courtesy and care by your staff? Are staff members offering them valuable information about relevant health concerns? Are they being entertained, rather than getting bored and frustrated? Are they being offered coffee or tea? Are you using that time to grow your practice by promoting new initiatives or referrals? As you'll read in Chapter 8, this window of time in the waiting room can be important for enhancing profitability. Most offices don't think about the waiting room as an opportunity to improve the patient's experience or create new value, and that's a mistake. Leveraging the waiting room is a simple example of what it means to upscale.

More broadly, upscaling means moving your practice up the value chain, and that applies to a great deal more than the waiting room. Let's say your practice currently offers only primary-care services, and you decide to bring in a cardiologist, a gynecologist, and a podiatrist. Or perhaps you decide to expand into ultrasounds and echocardiograms, or to do your own blood draws or iron infusions. Maybe you add an enrichment center to your practice, a place where patients can educate themselves about their health conditions. Perhaps you add a dispensary, so that patients are collecting their medications on-site. Suddenly you've made your practice more valuable to your patients because they no longer need to travel elsewhere for these specialty services. This is the essence of upscaling.

This may call to mind the work you did to create your Action Plan back in Chapter 3 because some of the same questions are as relevant here as in that planning process. How do you decide which services to add to your practice? How do you determine the best order in which to add them? It is only by gaining the time and perspective to step back from the practice of medicine, to see your practice as a business, that you can best make these decisions. This is why Part One of this book helped you to build the practice and personal base from which you can invest a portion of your work in the A-level strategic decisions of where to take your practice as well as the precise pathway for doing so.

In essence, upscaling is the cumulative impact of the intentional and deliberate steps that you've taken over time to enhance your practice's value to your patient base and to your medical community. Over time, a winning owner-independent practice needs to develop its own niche with its own suite of services that reflects its core practice vision.

In the next chapter you'll learn how to accelerate this crucial process— by engaging your team to build with you.

6

Accelerator Two: Engage Your Team

D oes developing your UBS, executing on your one-page quarterly Action Plan, and strengthening your practice's core, sound like a lot of work? It is. But here is the best-kept secret for how the physicians you're reading about in this book were able to both grow their practices and radically reduce their working hours: They employed practice Accelerator Two, and engaged their team in the process.

When Dr. Lara, owner of a successful four-clinic weight-management practice, first joined David's business-coaching program, he did something very smart. From the beginning of his participation in the program, he engaged four of his key practice managers and leaders in the program as well. That meant that, rather than Dr. Lara teaching his team to create his practice's UBS, he brought these four capable team members to the Systems and Controls workshop that David's company puts on each year, and he had them learn directly from David's team.

Those team members then left the workshop with a draft of their UBS completed, and a clear ninety-day Action Plan to take those all-important first steps toward building their practice systems. And knowing that coaching and mentoring his staff wasn't his strong suit, Dr. Lara had David's team coach his key managers directly, giving them monthly feedback and guidance to advance the practice. What this meant was, his *staff* was doing the heavy lifting and owning much of the growth process of improving his practice. It wasn't all on his shoulders.

Remember back in Chapter 1 when we encouraged you to make building an owner-independent practice a stated goal? We shared how this provided opportunities for your team to grow professionally, to have a greater contribution and bigger impact on the practice, and to enjoy greater job security. Accelerator Two says stop trying to do it all yourself; give your team a voice and a stake in doing the key work *with* you.

Why "Top Down" Doesn't Work

Two years after he founded Access Health Care, Dr. Singh gathered his leadership team for a meeting. When they were all assembled, he shared with them his ambition for their practice, which was, he said, "a quantum leap in health care." Dr. Singh aspired to five-star quality scores, empowered patients, near 100 percent patient satisfaction, near 100 percent operational efficiency, and better health outcomes. But when Dr. Singh told his leadership team that he had a vision for "a quantum leap in health care," how many people on the team do you think agreed with him?

The answer? Not one. Not a single person on the team that he had assembled to run the health-care company he had founded was interested in his vision for Access.

"So then we argued, we wrestled with one another, we went back and forth, back and forth, and we never really could agree," he says now, reflecting back on that time.

Their overall vision remained a point of contention for years, and in that time Dr. Singh gave up on trying to articulate a vision for the company—because it never got him anywhere. For a while he even thought it might not be necessary to have an overall vision.

And then, at last, he made the decision to bring in an outside coach to facilitate a strategic-planning retreat for his leadership team.

"Let's talk about where we want to take Access Health Care," said the coach, addressing the fifteen-person team that had assembled for the workshop. "What are your thoughts?" Notice that his coach didn't start by asking Dr. Singh for *his* vision; instead, he started out by asking Dr. Singh's team for *their* input. "Where do you think we should we take Access? What kind of future for the company excites you? What big goals do you think we should set for the practice?" he asked each person in turn.

So members of the leadership team started sharing their ideas. One person said she thought that every office should be a patient-centered medical home. It was a lofty goal, and one that would require a great deal of work.

Dr. Singh was surprised. He wasn't surprised that this member of his team held such a high goal for the company, but rather that she appeared to be saying the same thing he'd been saying all along. Turning every office into a patient-centered medical home would mean excellent patient engagement, good communication, high-quality care, and evidence-based medicine. It was everything that Dr. Singh had wanted, though she was saying it in a different way.

Then another person chimed in.

"OK, yes, PCMH. But level three," said this next person.

Since a level three PCMH implies the highest complexity of care, Dr. Singh was once again impressed. The meeting had just begun, but already his team was articulating a sterling vision.

Other team members chimed in. They began to discuss a timeline. Since there's a great deal of paperwork associated with filing for the PCMH designation, the team sketched out an implementation plan, and then assigned a specific person with bottom-line responsibility. They decided that they wanted to have three offices under the new designation within six months. And by the end of three years, they said, every single Access office would become a PCMH facility. That was a very big deal.

Nor did it stop there. Their coach continued to solicit ideas on other topics. On the question of quality of care, Access's chief quality officer said, "I would like for us to hit five stars this year."

That was the exact same goal that Dr. Singh had wanted. Together, the group set a goal of attaining a five-star rating within a year, and assigned responsibility for reaching that goal to one key team member.

Their coach continued to guide the team on topics of utilization management, IT, digital strategy, inventory—everything. One by one, everyone's specialty was brought up and addressed, and everybody had their goals. By the end, they had put it all together into one comprehensive plan. Now they had something that was everybody's vision; everyone was a stakeholder, and everyone knew what they wanted the company to be.

The process didn't end there. Quarter by quarter, their coach was in contact with each leader about the particular aspect of the plan that he or she owned. He emailed the chief quality officer to inquire about quality scores. He checked in with the appropriate person about the PCMH designation. And as they moved forward, everyone was kept current on everyone else's progress because it was progress toward their joint goals. If there was a failure in reaching a goal, then everyone knew the cause. It was openly shared and addressed, because everyone was a stakeholder.

The energy at Access changed after that. Suddenly everyone made concerted efforts to help one another, and they were all focused on shared success because they considered themselves owners of a collective vision. It wasn't some vision handed down from on high, but, rather, an emergent vision that they had a real voice in articulating.

It was at that meeting that Dr. Singh gleaned his single most important lesson about leading his organization. It's a lesson that has been crucial for much of his success since then: "If it's top down, it won't work. It's got to be bottom up," he says now. "Everyone on the team needs to have ownership."

On that single day, the company went from having one person in the top leadership role to fifteen people devoting themselves to formulating an ambitious vision.

Give Your Team a Real Voice

From the very first page, this book has been focused on helping you move in the direction of a particular goal: making your practice owner independent. But our insistence that your practice operate independently of your direct efforts—and independently of the efforts of any single person—doesn't mean that your people are unimportant. On the contrary, the only way to build an owner-independent Level Three practice is to have great team members who consistently dedicate themselves to their work.

So stop for a moment and take an honest look at your practice. Have you built and developed the kind of team that could, with the proper systems, handle day-to-day operations in your absence? Have you helped your team members build their individual confidence such that they could "own" parts of the practice? Do they feel empowered to make appropriate decisions and take necessary actions without running everything past you first?

Dr. Singh had a vision for what his practice should look like. But when he communicated it to his staff, not a single soul agreed with him. In contrast, when he gave the team a chance to build that vision together, they crafted something that was everything he had hoped for and more.

An engaged team that feels invested in the future of your practice is a necessary ingredient for building a Level Three owner-independent practice. And to achieve that degree of team engagement, your team members *must* have a meaningful voice in the process of growing your practice.

Giving your team a real voice means that you ask for their help and meaningful participation in this work of growing the practice. It means asking them for their thoughts, ideas, and feedback. And it means listening to their answers and giving their ideas real consideration. Whether you agree with their ideas or perspectives doesn't matter; the central idea is that you must give them respect and a seat at the table. Through this approach you'll gain a much deeper buy-in and commitment level from team members, no matter the ultimate vision and strategic plan you collectively agree on for the practice. Remember, you don't just need your team members' hands to do the work; you need their heads and hearts too.

Once you begin to seek staff input for a shared vision of the future, you may well be surprised by what you find. And, like Dr. Singh, you'll never want to go back to the old approach of top-down decision making. You will have found something much more powerful.

Connect Personal Goals to Practice Goals

Once your team has developed a collective vision, the next step is to link your shared goals for the overall practice with personal and departmental goals. In Dr. Singh's example, the leader of every department held a vision for what success at the company should look like. Of course, each one of those leaders also had a sense of what success personally looked like for him or her. And we're not talking about just professional success within the medical practice, but also connecting the practice, departmental, and professional goals to their individual life goals.

Let's say that you've finally reached your longtime goal of hiring another physician to expand your clinical capacity. You're now relying on this new doctor to relieve some of your patient load and free up some of your time. That's wonderful. In order to effectively engage this new physician and persuade her to truly dedicate her talents to the practice, you'll need to have a sense of the personal goals that are driving her. What are her ideas of success?

It's possible that her vision of success is to work three days a week instead of five. Maybe she has children and wants to spend more time with them. You may not be able to accommodate that right now—but what about in three years? What if you collaboratively grow the practice sufficiently over the next three years, then hire another doc, and suddenly this current doc can cut back to three days a week? Now you've got a shared goal, and a physician who is deeply invested in your joint success.

Don't stop there. Just as you did in Chapter 3 with your Action Plan, use that shared goal to get very specific about how much you need your practice to grow over the next three years to make that vision a reality. How many patients will your new provider need to add to her patient load each year in order to reach the goal by year three? Now work backward. How many patients will you need to add in year two? In year one? Over the next ninety days?

Write it down. Put it into the Action Plan. Break it down into chunks in the way that we described in Chapter 3. Assign chunks to the appropriate people. Assign metrics to those chunks, so that you track progress on a quarterly and then yearly basis. Now, as a team, you're moving systematically toward your goals. Your team, not just you, will now be driving this forward movement.

This does not apply only to your top-level providers. It also applies to the people in the front office. It applies to the people in the back office. And it applies to the mid-levels, who are doing the important work of helping to make your practice more efficient.

Free Yourself by Empowering Your Team

As your team sets shared goals and then breaks down the associated work into smaller chunks, you'll be tempted to tell them exactly how they should meet each of their goals. Resist the temptation. Instead of *telling* your team members, *ask* them.

"Knowing that this is your goal, what are your initial thoughts on how you'll accomplish this? Why don't you come up with a draft Action Plan, and we'll go over it together?"

See more in them than they see in themselves. They may be totally ready for it, or they may not be. Either way, let them do it—because that's how you encourage people to rise to their potential. And that's how you'll build something much greater than the outcome of any single task. It is how you'll build a practice that will, eventually, run on its own, without your day-to-day presence.

It won't happen all at once. Remember that this work is more like a dimmer knob that you turn gradually to make things brighter, rather than a light switch that you simply flick to the "on" position. By entrusting any given task to a team member rather than doing it yourself, you're freeing yourself just a little bit. And eventually, one day, it will take you by surprise: The whole operation hums without you.

Engaging your team in this way is only truly possible if team members are working within a constructive professional culture. Your practice's culture may seem like an intangible, something that's hard to intentionally shape and build. In fact, it's entirely possible to shape your practice's culture in simple, specific ways.

How do you go about that? Proceed to the next chapter to find out.

Accelerator Three: Cultivate Your Culture

ake their day. That's the motto that Dr. Challa calls, simply, "the
fish philosophy," because it has its origins in the Pike Place Fish
Market in Seattle. You might ask, "Make *whose* day?" The answer
is simple: Make your colleague's day, or your boss's day, or your employee's day, but most importantly, make your patient's day. *Make their
day* refers to all of the above.

When Dr. Challa first joined David's business-coaching program, his
practice was already a mature and successful organization. For that reason, some of his key people expressed surprise when he told them that he
was bringing on a coach to help guide the practice's continued growth.
These staff members believed that since Kansas Medical Clinic was by
all outward measures already very successful, they didn't need any
coaching.

Yet Dr. Challa understood that the success of his practice was not a static matter. In particular, he had always been a big believer in the importance of culture, and over the years, KMC had participated in a number of
different initiatives to shape its culture in positive ways. But Dr. Challa
had found that such initiatives always wore off after a couple of years.
That led him to focus on developing KMC's culture from several different angles, including by incorporating the *Make Their Day* philosophy
into their daily work.

Indeed, Dr. Challa and his team of providers have embedded this philosophy into the KMC culture in a very practical way. They use the
sticky-note function in their electronic chart software to log personal details about each patient, so that a provider can always take a moment to
ask a patient about something that matters on a personal level.

"How's your granddaughter Erin's basketball going?" Dr. Challa will ask, as he sits in the exam room across from an elderly patient. In response, the patient's face lights up, both because she now gets to talk about her favorite subject—her granddaughter—and because her doctor remembered a detail that she'd told him six months ago. Dr. Challa is the busiest gastroenterologist in the state of Kansas, but that doesn't keep him from checking in on each patient in a personal way. Over time, and with this sticky-note habit as a matter of routine policy, *Make Their Day* has become the prevailing philosophy throughout Kansas Medical Clinic. It is not only the guideline for how providers treat patients, but also for how all staff members treat one another.

Dr. Challa and his leadership team have also made the *Make Their Day* philosophy into one part of a much larger campaign to enhance culture. Every employee now receives a booklet called *The Great Philosophy*, which provides specific guidelines and tips for maintaining positivity, as well as encouragement on such matters as taking care of one another, taking breaks for rejuvenation, avoiding the vortex of workplace drama, and following the slogan "Play, within reason," which encourages spontaneity.

The result? An upbeat culture across KMC's nine locations. Every workplace has its difficulties, of course, and KMC is no different. But Dr. Challa has fostered in his organization the kind of positive environment where employees feel valued and can genuinely enjoy their workday together.

True to form, Dr. Challa gives all the credit for this success to his top HR person, Sonya, who he says is "the best HR person we've ever had."

The Hidden Hand That Shapes Your Team's Behavior

Up to this point in the book, we've been talking primarily about creating systems and internal controls that will eventually allow your practice to be owner independent. This matter of culture may seem to be a bit of a divergence from those earlier topics; after all, culture is a "softer" ingredient than, for instance, the hierarchy of folders that you use to organize your practice's UBS, or how you make strategic hires to grow your clinical capacity.

But your culture is a powerful accelerator to building an owner-independent practice that can function effectively and efficiently when you're not around. What happens when a novel situation comes up for which you don't have a system to determine how your team should respond? This is where your culture can save the day.

Your practice's culture is the combination of the absorbed values, implicit priorities, and unstated "way we do things around here." Culture is the invisible hand that shapes your team's behavior when no one is looking. It's what allows your team to handle new situations for which you have no designated system.

Cultivating a positive culture at your practice is a matter of two key ingredients. The first is your own personal behavior. What sort of conduct do you model for your team? This is especially relevant in tough moments. When a challenge arises, when it would be easy to get upset or cut corners, how do you behave? Since you're the leader, many of your employees will simply follow your lead in how they deal both with their day-to-day responsibilities and with sticky dilemmas.

The second key ingredient to cultivating positive culture is the shared values that you directly emphasize. When a team member performs in an exemplary fashion, do you praise that person both in private and in front of others? When someone acts in a way that's negative or inappropriate, do you address it, or do you just let it slide? If your team sees you tolerate bad behavior, you're effectively spoiling your culture.

But if you instead deal directly with negativity and other problems, and have the tough adult conversations that situations demand, then you're sending a clear message about what does and does not fly in your workplace. And if you consider the importance of this message in light of the fact that your own behavior is the first example that others will follow, it also becomes clear that owning and acknowledging your own missteps sets the best example for your team.

Ready to invest in your practice's vital culture? Here are six tips to help you do just that.

Six Tips for Establishing and Reinforcing Positive Culture

1. Write down your vision.

Write out a concrete vision of your practice's culture. Before you can establish your culture, let alone reinforce it, you need to become clear about what you want your culture to be.

What, ideally, do you want your practice culture to look like? What values do you want your team to internalize? How should these internalized values show up in staff behavior? What would an outside observer notice about your practice if he or she spent a day in your offices?

Gut Check: How does your practice currently line up with your vision of what you want your culture to be? Imagine once again that you're an outsider looking in. Where would you notice things aligning and not aligning between the observed culture and your desired culture?

Take this feedback and use it to refine your written vision of your practice. Then set aside time to talk with your team members about this vision. Get their thoughts and input. Just like the UBS, this is a process that unfolds over several months, not as a result of a one-time effort.

2. **Celebrate victories that align with your core values.**

Highlight great behavior; celebrate successes. This reinforces the values that you want your team to hold, and over time, these small steps of praise and celebration accumulate to establish your culture. Consider sending out a company-wide email retelling the story of a particular victory, or highlighting it at a meeting.

Dr. Challa's HR manager, Sonya, gathers success stories into a monthly newsletter called the "Great Email." Here's how Sonya describes it: "We focus on the employee by recognizing superior performance and celebrating achievements both work-related and personal, in order to build morale. It is a newsletter for them and about them, and it lets them and their peers know how important they are to KMC." Every "Great Email" that KMC sends out celebrates exemplary employee performance, and it does so under the culture-reinforcing headline of "No Drama—We are Family—Make the Patient's Day—Play."

You get the idea: reinforce key values and behaviors that you want other people to internalize.

3. **Look for small stories that symbolize deeper meaning.**

You don't need to highlight only victories. Also take the time to look for small occurrences that symbolize the deeper values you want your team to absorb. For example, if Carol came in on Saturday to check on a patient who had a poor reaction to a medication, and you want that same degree of diligence and care to become a core value, then publicly thank Carol for it. Ask her how it went and what she learned, and then share those insights with your whole team—which, of course, allows you to subtly retell the underlying story of Carol caring enough to check on a patient on a Saturday.

4. **Intentionally make the hard decision.**

   This might mean ending an alliance with another practice that doesn't fit with the direction and mission of your own office, or publicly accepting responsibility for a poor decision, or shutting down a failed project. Your team needs to see you model and live your culture. They're watching closely—even if you don't realize it.

5. **Start with recruitment.**

   Emphasize your values and culture in your hiring, selection, and orientation of new team members. Build into your hiring process checks for the personality and values that will directly align with the culture you want. When you bring on a new hire, make sure that you communicate the values of your practice, not just with a ten-minute talk, but, rather, by having multiple people share stories and experiences to make those values and culture real.

6. **Cull your low performers.**

   If you want high performance and personal responsibility to be integral parts of your culture, you've got to cull your low performers now. Every medical practice (and every other type of workplace) has them: those team members who everyone knows are just getting by. If you give them a pass by not dealing with their poor performance, then the message you're sending to the rest of your team is that weak behavior is acceptable.

   Your high performers will also find the presence of deadweight on the team to be demotivating. Why should they work hard when others are just sliding by? For this reason it's especially crucial to cull your low performers now, and replace them with better and better people. Yes, this might cause some short-term pain, but the long-term rewards are worth it. "I think of it as upgrading the team," says Dr. Challa. "You lose somebody, and then you gain somebody who's better."

At the Kansas Medical Clinic, Dr. Challa and his team have added a new habit as part of their drive to build positive culture: Every patient now receives a handwritten note from their nurse. Recently, one patient submitted a comment card that specifically mentioned the note that she'd received, declaring, "What a great staff!" Of course, this success story was then included by the HR team in the next month's

"Great Email," along with an affirmation: "Way to make the patient's day!"

Positive culture doesn't just build morale; it's also a matter of your bottom line. When your practice boasts a positive work environment, your employee retention will improve—because great people want to continue working in a great environment. That will save you money, of course, because turnover is costly, and that, in turn, improves your overall profitability. For more essential tips on enhancing profitability, turn to the next chapter.

CHAPTER 8

Accelerator Four: Enhance Your Profitability

D r. Kim's dental practice spent a small fortune on marketing efforts that were supposed to bring in a steady flow of patients. When she actually ran the numbers, however, she found that she was paying a huge amount for each new patient.

Then she began working with David's coaching team, and she started thinking strategically about ways to increase her patient volume without breaking the bank. She thought about the army of patients she'd seen over the years for various procedures who did not return on a regular basis for routine cleanings and exams. Soon Dr. Kim began developing an internal process for reactivating those patients. Once a month, a member of her staff pulled the records of patients who had not been in for nine months or more. Her business coach, in collaboration with her two clinics' office managers, developed a simple script to bring these lapsed patients back in for an exam and cleaning.

"Hi, Krista. This is Ron from Cottage Dental. Dr. Kim asked me to reach out to you. It's been almost a year since your last exam, and she is concerned about your oral health. There was a study published in the *New England Journal of Medicine* showing the link between low-grade oral infection and your risk of heart disease, and Dr. Kim wants me to schedule you for your next appointment. Is this week or next week better for you?"

This simple script gave them a powerful way to inexpensively increase their patient volume, and it yielded dramatic results. A quarter of the people they contacted immediately booked an appointment for an exam.

With calls to lapsed patients now a standard procedure at Dr. Kim's office, she has consistently improved her patient volume. This successful reactivation strategy allowed her to cut several of her other expensive marketing strategies that weren't delivering results. Not only did she increase her patient volume at her two clinics by 12 and 32 percent respectively, but also, her practice now had a proactive way to influence the consistency of patient volume due to the number of outbound reactivation calls her staff made in any given week.

And that's the very heart of this chapter. In the pages ahead, you'll find a series of simple, proven strategies to improve profitability. Remember, as the owner of a medical practice, you have three primary ways to improve your profitability:

- **Reduce expenses.**
- **Enhance revenues.**
- **Improve billing collections.**

The following tips will leverage each of these approaches in a variety of ways. Let's get started.

Twelve Vital Tips for Enhancing Your Practice's Profitability

1. Know your financials.
When you're trying to understand a patient's health status, one of the first things you do is check their vital signs. When it comes to enhancing your profitability, keeping a close eye on your practice's financials is just as important. Indeed, the doctors who are on top of their financial statements are the ones who run economically successful practices. Of course, the reality is that you likely never took a class in medical school on understanding financial statements; instead, you've had to learn it on your own. It's no wonder so many doctors simply ignore—or at the very least, undermanage—this critical part of their practice.

But you can become financially savvy and understand your financials. The way to develop financial fluency is, simply, to have consistent exposure to your numbers. Make it a habit of sitting down with your controller, CPA, or business coach each month to look at your practice's financial statements. Ask a lot of questions. This will initially feel uncomfortable—precisely because, right now, you're probably unfamiliar with the material. Once you get the hang of it, though, you'll feel a lot more comfortable, and, eventually, going over last month's numbers will take no more than thirty minutes. From now on, commit to reviewing each month's numbers *by no later than the end of the next month*. Don't let them linger until next quarter (or worse, until they're too old to bother looking at all!).

As you grow more confident with your numbers, you'll begin to spot easy ways to enhance your profitability. As just one example, consider your marketing expenses. Do you know how well your main lead-generation activities perform? Do you know your cost per lead? Once you have good numerical data, you can stop wasting money—as Dr. Kim did—on below-average efforts, and instead, invest in the things that really work. And that leads us right into tip number two.

Turn Around an Underperforming Practice Area and See How It Increases Your Bottom Line

You might remember that, back in Chapter 1, we wrote about Dr. Landon, a surgeon based in Florida. We described his exhausting schedule, and the fact that his practice was always deeply dependent on his personal efforts. Well, Dr. Landon wasn't just working too much and wearing himself out. He was also developing his practice in ways that weren't always profitable. In fact, one area of his practice was deeply in the red—but he didn't realize it.

"We doctors tend to get immersed in the work of dealing with patients, and I think we're often divorced from the day-to-day fiduciary responsibility of the office," he says now. Just after he'd started working with David's team, they did a deep dive into the financials—and discovered that the medical spa component of his surgery practice was losing $100,000 each year.

Working with Dr. Landon's team, they immediately made a few key changes, including reducing administrative staff associated with the spa and raising prices to properly reflect the cost of service. "Within about four months, the spa went from being $100,000 in the hole to being a $150,000-a-year winner," he says—and you can hear the relief in his voice.

2. Feed Your Winners; Starve Your Losers.

Once you're on top of your numbers, you can start to get very strategic about which activities you invest in, and which you stop doing altogether. That's exactly what Dr. Kim was doing when she cut the marketing tactics that were costly and ineffective, and invested instead in a low-cost, high-impact reactivation strategy.

Right now you're probably doing some marketing and promotional activities that work exceptionally well. These are your winners. At the same time, some of your marketing tactics probably create very little value and fail to justify their cost. These are your losers. It's time to "starve" those losers. Take the bottom 30 or 40 percent, stop doing them, and reinvest that time and money into your winners, the top 10 or 20 percent of marketing activities that are really performing. That is, feed your winners and starve your losers. As with cutting D-level activities and reinvesting your time into A- and B-level work, you'll find that you get phenomenal results from taking this approach.

This strategy doesn't apply only to your marketing efforts, of course. It applies to your staff, your patient types, and your service lines. For example, which service areas of your practice are highly profitable? And which are marginally profitable or even losing money? Once you've answered those questions, it's time to feed your winners and starve your losers. As Dr. Landon discovered, all it took was a few changes to his medical spa to push that area of his practice well into the black.

3. Increase patient volume.

Patient volume is an absolutely critical part of enhancing your practice's profitability. While we don't have space in this chapter to address every strategy we'd like to share, we will cover some of the big ones. We've also recorded a powerful training video on other ways to increase patient volume, and you and your staff can access that video and the other practice tools at **www.GrowMyMedicalPractice.com**. (See Appendix A for full details.)

- Pay attention to your conversion rate, the percentage of potential new patients who actually make appointments and show up. If people are calling your office to make an appointment and can't get through immediately—if they get put on hold, or otherwise have to wait for service—you're probably losing potential patients, and perhaps a great number of them. Start counting how many calls are live-answered and how many are placed on hold. What percentage of these calls end in a new patient showing up in your office? Con-

Dr. Padda's World-Class Customer Service

Dr. Padda is serious about customer service. So serious, in fact, that his practice never misses a single call from a patient, and every call is answered in *less than half a second*. That might sound impossible, but it makes perfect sense once you understand his strategy.

"I took my entire call-answering department and moved it to the Philippines," he explains. "They have my scheduler on their systems. I train them, and they know the right questions to ask, and they put the patients right into the schedule."

This approach didn't just deliver better service for his patients, whose every call is answered in an astonishing .15 seconds. It also saved him a ton of money, because the going wage for this work in the Philippines is a small fraction of what it is in the United States (to be clear, he's paying his overseas workers what they consider to be a good salary). And with that savings, Dr. Padda invested yet again in his customer service.

"I've got staff who've been with me for twelve years, and they're the highest-paid front-desk staff in the city. I pay them effectively two times the going rate because they do the job of two-and-a-half people. My people here in the United States are dealing with patients directly, face-to-face, and they themselves are the marketers."

Even after taking into account the higher wages of his front-office staff, this arrangement still saves Dr. Padda money—and it has delivered remarkable results. His practice never loses a prospective patient who calls for an appointment. Meanwhile, patients in the office are delighted with the top-quality service and care they receive. That's how Dr. Padda has built his practice into seven highly successful medical clinics across the state of Missouri.

sider hiring another person just for the phones, or you may even want to consider a strategy like Dr. Padda's.

■ Focus on how well you **retain patients**. It's far better and more cost effective to retain an existing patient than to attract a new one. Keep in mind the **lifetime value** of each patient (and if you don't know this number, then sit down with your CFO, CPA, or business coach to help you calculate it), and act accordingly. Design your customer-service efforts with the specific goal of keeping patients happy

("Make their day," as Dr. Challa would say) and keeping them at your practice. As with boosting your conversion rate, your front-office phone service is critical for retaining patients.

■ A **reactivation strategy** like the one that Dr. Kim used may prove invaluable for your practice. Consider devising an approach that relates specifically to your area of medicine. For example, in Dr. Lara's weight-loss practice it's extremely common for patients to see huge improvements within a few months, and then to backslide over the next twelve to twenty-four months after leaving treatment. Dr. Lara's particular reactivation strategy is a matter of calling patients to check in on their progress. If patients are once again struggling with their weight, they're invited to come back for another appointment and ongoing support to maintain their ideal weight and a healthy lifestyle.

■ Launch a **referral program**. Once again, consider tailoring your approach to your particular practice area. As an example, consider the chiropractor in San Diego who specialized in serving runners and other athletes. A lot of runners belong to local running clubs and compete regularly in road races, so this doctor began encouraging

Dr. Challa's "Friends and Family" Program

Dr. Challa routinely spent a couple hundred thousand dollars every year on marketing. Then, as he describes it, "Suddenly I woke up one day and said, 'We're not going after the Low-Hanging Fruit!'" That was when he and his team began their Friends and Family program. If you walk into an office of the Kansas Medical Clinic today, you'll see a poster that proudly states, "Our patients think we are great!" It includes several endorsements from patients, and a message that encourages patients to refer their own friends and family members to the practice.

Dr. Challa didn't stop there, though. When he opened a new dermatology clinic, he hosted a private event at the new clinic specifically geared toward the friends and family of existing patients. For one day only, the new dermatology office offered free screenings for friends and family members—and, in the process, they picked up nearly fifty new patients. That's a huge win, especially when you consider that it often takes a new office more than a year to fill up its schedule, which translates into months of paying providers for sometimes empty schedules.

his patients to refer other athletes. Eventually he became the go-to provider for runners across the San Diego area.

■ Consider a **cross-promotion** strategy. One GI doctor, for instance, had the following powerful realization: Every single patient arrived at his office accompanied by someone who would drive him or her home after the procedure—a fact that could serve as a major recruitment opportunity. He began instructing his staff to ask the accompanying friend or family member if he or she was aware of the importance of screening colonoscopies for people over age fifty, and inviting that individual to come in for an appointment. Just one month after putting this new strategy into effect, they had recruited ten new patients.

4. Leverage your lower-cost providers.

We've already emphasized the importance of expanding your team in order to free up your valuable time. Adding a mid-level provider creates additional direct revenue as that individual starts seeing his or her own patients, and it creates indirect revenue by giving you back 10 percent of your time to reinvest in your highest-value work.

But there are other advantages to increasing your use of mid-level providers. Consider once again Dr. Lara and his weight-loss clinic. Over time, Dr. Lara had developed a very effective approach to weight loss. And though he had tried employing staff physicians to handle some of his patient load, he had a great deal of trouble convincing these physicians to follow his proven protocol and treatment philosophy. Eventually Dr. Lara switched from physicians to nurse practitioners— and, lo and behold, patients actually received better results. Unlike the staff physicians, he found that the nurse practitioners were open to learning and utilizing Dr. Lara's approach. At the same time, he reduced his payroll cost by 50 percent for each position, and saw improvements in his culture.

5. Renegotiate your costs.

Don't be afraid to renegotiate expenses. When in doubt, bid it out. Prices that may seem fixed and inflexible often turn out to be quite the opposite. As your practice grows, you have more negotiating leverage. But even without such leverage, an effective negotiator can often end up scoring a better deal. At Dr. Singh's practice, one staff member embraced this challenge and struck a new and better deal with the sanitation company that hauled away their biowaste. She also negotiated a better arrangement with the company that handled their medical records. This is a skill set worth investing in, so consider letting a member of your staff attend a seminar or two on negotiation; that's a cost that will pay for itself several times over.

You may also be suffering from what we call the "ZIP code problem." Some contractors will look at your address—or the letters after your name—and add a premium to their price. So go ahead and let them know that you have other companies bidding for the same contract. You might be surprised to find that that alone knocks 10 or 15 percent right off the top.

6. Optimize your space.

Your physical space matters both for increasing revenue and for controlling expenses—because space is money. Every inch of your office can be utilized, though it may take a bit of creativity to figure out how to do so. Sometimes a tweak here and there is enough to create two additional exam rooms from what was previously a storage area. Storage can go outside or even off-site; your premium space should be reserved for producing medical services.

One of Dr. Singh's clinics started out as just a tiny, 1,600-square-foot office. Thanks to a great staff physician, however, that clinic grew quickly, and they soon took over the unit next door, adding another 1,600 square feet. Then they added yet another unit. At that point, the office was basically three separate spaces connected by small doorways. Every time the physician came out of an exam room, she spent forty-five seconds walking the hallway looking for an MA to finish with the patient. She wasted these forty-five seconds at the end of every appointment.

So what did they do? Eventually they dedicated a low-level staff person exclusively to that physician, an arrangement that ended up saving the doc enough time that she could see a two more patients every day. Not only did this increase the clinic's profits, but it also helped them retain that employed physician.

7. Centralize your scheduling.

While you may not be ready to take the leap that Dr. Padda did to move your scheduling offshore, it's at least essential that you centralize the scheduling for all of your offices into one place. David's company currently works with a physician whose practice has four locations and is in the process of building a fifth. Rather than having the staff at each office take calls to schedule appointments, they've centralized their scheduling at a single location. Thanks to the efficiency of that move, they've been able to extend their hours and hire additional staff to make sure that every call gets a live answer. In addition to reducing overhead, this will up your conversion rate because you won't be losing prospective patients by missing their calls, and a centralized call center with dedicated staff is easier to manage and train.

8. Batch similar procedures together.

For just a moment, imagine your medical practice as a kind of assembly line. Will this assembly line work most efficiently if it constantly changes up the fixtures and machinery to alternatively produce one product and then another, different product? Of course not. And while we know that a medical practice is not precisely akin to an assembly line, there are aspects of business management and supply economics that can be applied here with significant effect. In this case, you've got to be strategic about when you produce which services. The time and energy required to set up for any given procedure is almost always significant, and in many cases it's two-thirds of the entire time required for that procedure. So start batching like procedures back-to-back in your schedule, rather than scattering them throughout the week. That way, you and your staff won't need to reset for each appointment; you can do it all in one fell swoop, and save a considerable amount of time and money in the process.

Dr. Padda's Approach to Drug Reps

Those hours spent talking with pharmaceutical reps can be an expensive use of time at any medical practice. After observing the cost associated with all this drained time, Dr. Padda developed a hardline solution.

"While a sales rep is trying to sell you something, you're losing $1,600 an hour, because you're not using that time to treat patients," says Dr. Padda. "That's why we don't permit sales reps in our clinics. If somebody wants to give us information, we expect it to be written information. That's it. We don't do lunches, dinners, or meetings."

9. Stagger your staff.

There's no reason your practice has to be open from eight o'clock in the morning to five o'clock in the evening Monday through Friday and closed at all other times. If you're limited by clinical capacity, consider staying open until seven on certain days, or opening on Saturday (without your being physically present).

David recently worked with a medical practice in Southern California that was badly constrained by its physical space—in particular, because real estate in the area is prohibitively expensive. So they started staggering staff, with some people coming in at the normal time and others arriving later, and keeping the practice open in the evening. As it turned out, their patients loved the flexibility. That practice is now open an impressive four evenings each week, and on Saturdays. More impressively, they've nearly doubled their revenue while keeping most of their overhead costs fixed.

Not only is this a win-win for your practice, but it may also be a huge positive for your staff. At Dr. Singh's practice, they have a team of hospitalists, many of whom are young and eager for additional work. Dr. Singh created a pool of these physicians to take off-hours ER calls, and these doctors earn incentive pay for doing so: They personally take home 60 percent of those collections. Dr. Singh's practice then pays about 6 percent to the billing company, which leaves a healthy 34 percent margin.

10. Add specialty testing to your practice.

Consider expanding your practice into specialty testing. A primary-care physician, for instance, can easily add services like vascular testing, echocardiograms, carotid Doppler, and a variety of other tests. Besides growing your revenue, this adds value for your patients—because suddenly they don't have to trek all over town.

11. Improve billing accuracy.

This is a big one. Billing accuracy can mean the difference between a highly successful practice and one that goes bankrupt. There are four primary places where billing accuracy comes into play:

- **Treatment:** Are you accurately recording services rendered at the time of care?

- **Checkout:** When patients leave your office, are they paying the appropriate co-pays or private-pay fees?

- **EMR Coding:** Are staff members and providers throughout your office using the right EMR codes? This is absolutely critical to improve compliance, reduce under-coding and over-coding, minimize accounts receivable, and reduce your number of denials. For managed care, validation of codes is also essential to avoid subsequent denials. Proper coding requires educating staff and providers—and it's well worth the investment.

- **Insurance:** Are you billing for the correct services in the correct volume?

■ **Collection Controls:** Do you collect your third-party-payer receivables on a timely basis? Are you receiving the correct amounts that you are owed? Can you qualify for higher reimbursement rates?

David's team recently worked with a medical group that discovered a whopping $75,000 in missed billing *over a single sixty-day period*. That's a surefire way to go broke. Make it a habit at your practice to regularly pull a report to determine whether there are claims just sitting in your system. Sometimes claims languish in the equivalent of your drafts box, and all it takes is one click to push them out.

12. Create financial controls.

We are now going to reveal perhaps the most frightening statistic that a physician will ever hear: An astonishing 82 percent of medical practices are victims of fraud or theft, according to a report conducted by the Medical Group Management Association in 2009. That is *twice* the national average for private companies. Effectively, this means you have a four-in-five chance of being defrauded or stolen from. In 18.4 percent of these cases, the amount taken was over $100,000.

This is why our final tip on enhancing practice profitability is practically a call to arms: You *must* create financial controls. The following are some examples:

■ One person on your staff should be responsible for tallying, while a second person should check the math and make the deposit.

■ One person in accounts payable should handle invoices and cut checks, while a second person should review and sign those checks before they're sent out.

■ The person who has the power to withdraw money from the bank account should not be the same person who reconciles that account.

■ No single staff member should have the ability to move funds between accounts *and* withdraw funds.

It's essential that your staff members perceive you as vigilant in regard to finances. One common way that employees steal is by putting expenses on credit cards or by creating false vendors. This is most likely to happen, of course, when the boss isn't paying close attention. Your staff members probably know whether or not you actually look at the credit card statements. At the very least, take those statements and mark them up—even if you don't really look at them closely. That suggests that you're keeping an eye on expenses.

Also, limit your potential losses. Perhaps $400,000 came in this month. Does that money then just sit in your operating account? Consider moving the surplus over what is needed for operations into a higher-order account—an account to which your staff does not have access.

If you do see something out of the ordinary, even if it's relatively small, make sure to question it right away. Don't do so in an aggressive fashion, of course, or in a way that blames anyone. Just question it, and get to the bottom of it. This shows your team that you're keeping watch.

External controls are also crucial. Last year, Dr. Singh's comptroller got an email from Dr. Singh saying that they needed to wire $20,000 to a vendor in Miami immediately. At their practice they have an internal guideline stating that the CFO and Dr. Singh must both approve wire transfers. In this case, since Dr. Singh was rushing it, the comptroller went ahead and initiated the wire—and then saw that the account was located in New York, not Miami. So he immediately emailed Dr. Singh to clarify. It's a good thing he did. Dr. Singh had never sent that email; their accounts had been hacked.

You're now well on your way to making your practice financially robust, even as it requires less and less of your own time and energy. Of course, even the best financial systems won't be enough to protect you from a worst-case scenario. And that's why the next chapter contains information essential to protecting yourself from lawsuits.

Accelerator Five: Protect Your Assets

According to a 2010 AMA report, more than 61 percent of doctors older than fifty-five have been sued at least once. Let's face it: The odds are not in your favor. Here you are, working so hard, investing the time and energy to grow and mature your practice, and yet, it could all be shaken or even destroyed in a lawsuit.

In this chapter, we'll lean heavily on Alan's thirty-three years of experience representing physicians and their medical practices. Dr. Singh and David like to refer to Alan as "the doctor's lawyer" because of his experience representing thousands of physicians in almost every conceivable situation. In this chapter you'll find his best input to help you protect yourself and your practice from lawsuits, creditors, and other potential threats.

Don't Let This Happen to You

Consider what happened to a physician we'll call Dr. Arneaux. He was in his late sixties and was getting ready to retire after he had put all of his children through private school. He had even worked a few more years than he'd intended in order to finally save enough for retirement. What he hadn't done, however, was take proper protective measures to plan for a worst-case event. When he called Alan's law office for help, he was facing a lawsuit from an angry patient. To make matters worse, several pages of the patient's chart had gone missing, perhaps stolen by Dr. Arneaux's former employee, who was a friend of the patient.

Worse still, the angry patient had hired a litigator who was known for aggressive tactics and had made a name for himself by suing doctors. He was known to browbeat physicians during their depositions, and he sometimes took lawsuits all the way to trial just for the publicity.

After two painful years of litigation, the matter was finally settled. Dr. Arneaux ended up having to write a sizeable check on top of the payment made by his malpractice-insurance carrier. He lost a lot of sleep in those two years, and the ordeal drained a significant amount of the honor and pride of the more than thirty-five years he had spent practicing medicine.

No one should have to go through that—at any age—and if you find this story terrifying, we understand. You're also not alone, not by a long stretch. The truth is that most doctors don't seriously plan for this scenario; only about 40 percent take the right precautions to protect themselves. And yet advance planning makes an enormous, and even a life-changing, difference. In Dr. Arneaux's case, the story would have had a different ending if only he had done a few key things beforehand. Once the patient had initiated legal action, Dr. Arneaux did everything in his power to protect himself from further harm. But certain precautions taken in advance would have made a huge difference.

The good news is that, if you act proactively, you can reduce the likelihood that you'll ever be sued, and you can build legal protections around your practice and personal assets to radically diminish the risk of losing anything significant if a lawsuit does occur. So let's get to work getting you protected.

Recognize Your Risks

The first step to protecting yourself is to concretely identify your top legal threats. Once you've recognized the sources of risk, you can then adequately protect yourself. Here are the top five legal risks you face as both a practicing physician and the owner of a medical practice:

Risk #1: Medical Malpractice for Acts and Omissions as a Practicing Physician

Malpractice can take many forms; among the most common is the failure to see a test and make a diagnosis, or the failure to notify a patient about an abnormal test result.

Risk #2: Medical Malpractice for the Acts and Omissions of Those Who Work for You

Remember, much of this liability falls to the practice entity and to you as the owner.

Risk #3: Medicare, Medicaid, and Insurance Carrier Suits and Infractions

These include suits and penalties related to billing and collections activities that are noncompliant with what are sometimes arcane and quite complex rules. Sadly, many of these suits are the result of employee whistle-blowers who were involved in the very violations they reported.

Risk #4: Liability for Car, Motorcycle, Boat, or Other Accidents

While it may seem as though this type of liability is not unique to doctors, in fact, people are more likely to sue when they learn that the operator of the other vehicle is a doctor; that is, they see a dollar sign on your head. You're also liable for the negligence of any driver operating a vehicle that contains your name on the title.

Risk #5: Ordinary Business Exposures

These exposures include the following: if someone slips and falls, if a patient or employee is mistreated or harassed by another employee, contract damage when a business dealing goes awry, liability from business or investment activities in your name or in the name of a company in which you serve as an officer or director, and liability for actions or inactions of a partner in a partnership that is not incorporated (all partners in a general partnership are jointly liable).

Many types of liabilities cannot be expunged through bankruptcy and will stay with you forever. These include some kinds of Medicare payback obligations and penalties, certain taxes, penalties associated with environmental waste, and malpractice in which the doctor was found reckless or willful in his or her conduct.

Thankfully, just by identifying the risks that threaten you and your practice, you've taken an important first step toward safeguarding your livelihood. The next step is to build the proper legal protections around you and your practice.

Powerful Protections to Put into Place *Before* You Get Sued

Now that you understand the risks, let's talk about what you can do to protect yourself, your practice, and your family.

Lawsuits are normally filed against both the doctor and the practice, and sometimes other affiliated entities as well. Many doctors erroneously assume that a lawsuit will settle within the limits of their malpractice insurance. This is incorrect. In fact, few plaintiff lawyers are willing to settle for policy limits unless both the doctor and the practice entity are what we call "judgment proof." What does it take to be judgment proof? You'll find that below, along with the rest of our list of key strategies for protecting yourself. (And for even more information on how to be judgment proof, we strongly encourage you to watch Alan's powerful video, "12 Asset Protection Strategies Every Physician Must Know to Reduce Their Personal and Practice Exposure." You can watch this video for free at **www.GrowMyMedicalPractice.com**. See Appendix A for full details.)

First, review your internal systems to make sure that your billing and other processes are compliant with medical law. Every medical practice should be able to document that it has relied on competent legal counsel or consultants hired through legal counsel under attorney/client privilege to confirm appropriate protocol, billing codes, and procedures. Indeed, a four- to eight-hour visit by a billing consultant not only reduces risk and increases compliance, but it can also enhance profitability and identify new billable services. A great many physicians are amazed to discover how many gaps existed in their billing practices—and how easily such problems can be resolved with the help of a competent consultant.

Also, consider whether you should eliminate certain high-risk procedures, patient categories, and problem patients entirely from your practice. In the case of problem patients, and thanks to the 80/20 rule that we discussed back in Chapter 2, we know that 80 percent of your problems will come from 20 percent of your patients. Part of protecting yourself from a lawsuit is considering whether a difficult patient is someone you want to continue treating. While it's important to take a dispassionate look at the feedback such patients provide—because they may be sharing a complaint that other patients have been too polite to raise—you may need to take action if you're dealing with someone who continually complains. Perhaps they don't belong at your practice. Consider terminating them.

If a patient does sue you, and if you are ordered to pay, we want your assets organized so there's nothing of value for the plaintiff's lawyer to take. Remember that even if you're found primarily not at fault, the cost can still be considerable. In one memorable case at Alan's firm, a jury found a doctor only "30 percent negligent," but the damages were assessed at $3 million—and 30 percent of $3 million is $900,000.

To avoid that nightmare, here are steps to make yourself, your family, and your practice judgment proof:

- Have the medical practice owe debt that is secured by liens filed in the public record, called UCC-1 Financing Statements. This debt should be almost as large as the value of the practice assets, including accounts receivable. If for any reason the practice can't borrow money, you can personally borrow from a friendly lender, such as parents or another family member, and have your medical practice guarantee the debt and pledge its assets as collateral. In the event of a judgment, the friendly creditor can repossess the collateral of the medical practice.

- Have valuable assets, like equipment and real estate, held outside of the medical practice in another entity. If your tax advisor tells you that this may trigger tax liability, get a second opinion from a corporate-tax expert and ask about something called "New Parent F Reorganization."

- If you own the building in which your practice operates, you can have it held by a separate LLC or other entity to shield you from liability if someone gets injured on-site. You can also have the owning entity owe a mortgage to the bank or family member and have the medical practice guarantee the mortgage and pledge its assets as collateral such that, if the practice suffers a judgment against it, that will serve as a violation of the loan covenants. The bank will then call in the loan and repossess the practice's assets, in which case there is nothing left for the plaintiff's lawyer.

- If you rent the building in which your practice operates, you can set up a twenty-year lease with the landlord company stating that, if the practice goes bankrupt, twenty years of rent is suddenly due, and the landlord has a lien to enforce it.

- Consider separating your practice into different companies. If you have a general practice and an urgent-care location, for instance, these could be distinct companies. Though they will likely need to be owned by a common parent company for Medicare billing purposes, this still creates a legal hurdle.

- Review all partnership and shareholder agreements, buy-sell agreements, life insurance, and disability insurance policies to ensure that they are properly situated and inaccessible to creditors.

- Understand and make use of assets that are creditor protected in your state (these vary significantly from state to state). Oftentimes a homestead, assets owned jointly as "tenants by the entireties with a spouse," annuity contracts, pensions, IRAs, and 529 college savings plans are protected. It is crucial to work with a lawyer who is familiar with the laws in your state.

- Consider holding valuable personal assets in your spouse's name to protect from creditors. Also consider a marital agreement in which your spouse pledges to put those assets into joint names, or as otherwise requested, in the event of a divorce.

- Consider employing your children. Since their IRAs are also protected from your creditors, you can employ your kids and pay them up to $5,500 a year, and put those wages into IRAs that may be creditor-proof for the entire lifetime of the child.

- Be strategic with how you pay yourself out of your practice. The most protected financial vehicle is a pension. Have a skilled actuary custom design your pension, and consider using a defined benefit plan or a cash balance plan to maximize contributions. Many states also provide for the protection of wages and investments purchased with wages, if state-specific rules are met.

- Consider using family limited partnerships, multiple-member LLCs, irrevocable trusts, and other vehicles that will protect assets from creditors.

- Properly structure any inheritances that may be coming your way. If you're expecting to inherit money from your parents, structure the inheritance so it will be paid into a trust for your benefit and not directly to you, in order to protect it from creditors. You can even serve as the trustee of the trust if it is properly drafted.

- Integrate the above with your personal estate and financial planning in order to ensure that you and your family are fully protected.

As you can easily imagine, the above items need to be carefully coordinated with the guidance of a qualified attorney and a certified public accountant. Be wary of advisors who are not attorneys but purport to give legal guidance. Many well-meaning, non-lawyer advisors who offer legal advice have caused significant harm. Make sure that any attorney you work with specializes in serving medical practices. To make sure you're getting someone who is genuinely qualified to do this high-stakes work, select a lawyer who is both board certified and has a peer rating of "AV" (the highest rating) in the Martindale-Hubbell legal directories. An attorney who has both of these qualifications is your best bet.

If You Get Sued

Once you've put the proper protections in place, a lawsuit is not the nightmare that it was for Dr. Arneaux. Getting sued will never be pleasant, but it doesn't have to be devastating.

Remember that the first step for you to take if you are ever served with a lawsuit or know that there is a real chance of one coming is to immediately get in contact with your attorney.

Consider what happened to Dr. Weiss, one of Alan's clients. Dr. Weiss was committed to planning ahead, so she'd had her practice and personal assets carefully organized so as to protect herself from creditors. When Dr. Weiss found out she was being sued, she didn't panic. But she also didn't initially call Alan and let him know what was happening. Instead, she made the unfortunate decision to rely on her insurance carrier's attorney. Perhaps she thought she was saving money, or maybe she believed that her malpractice carrier really had her best interests at heart, but the attorney assigned by the carrier was not the best defense lawyer around, and did not look carefully at the entire case. At the same time, the insurance carrier hired an outside expert who believed that Dr. Weiss was at least partly at fault.

After a year of depositions there was a mediation negotiation, and the plaintiff made a settlement offer—but the lawyer advised Dr. Weiss not to settle. He also failed to mention that, if they did settle, the insurance carrier alone would be responsible for any additional verdict in excess of the policy limits. In other words, settling at that stage would have entirely eliminated Dr. Weiss's exposure.

But by now, Dr. Weiss did realize that she needed her own attorney, and she called Alan's office. Horrified by the guidance she'd received, Alan called the plaintiff's lawyer. He explained that there was nothing to be gained by going to trial because Dr. Weiss was so well protected; even if she went bankrupt, the plaintiff would still get next to nothing. While Alan understood that Dr. Weiss was in a very strong negotiating position since she had done all the prior work to structure her affairs for maximum protection, he also knew that it was in Dr. Weiss's best interest to settle the lawsuit within the policy limits rather than go to trial. This is exactly what Alan pushed for and got to happen, thus ending the lawsuit.

For most doctors, this strategy would not have worked. But because Dr. Weiss had put in place such strong protections, she significantly limited the fear, stress, and financial harm from the lawsuit. We want this best-case outcome for you too.

Take Proper Action When Trouble Arises

If you learn that you're being sued—or even suspect that trouble may be on the horizon—don't stick your head in the sand. Start preparing by locating the patient's records and storing them in a safe place. Then revisit everything you remember about the situation. It's easy to think that you'll remember everything in two years, but you won't. Dictate a thorough memo while the situation is fresh. Don't change a patient's chart or even consider backdating anything without getting careful legal advice. Juries will punish perceived dishonesty by a doctor.

In some cases it also makes sense to have your staff interviewed. The CNA who was in the room with you may not work for you in six months (and she may be friends with the patient, as in the case of Dr. Arneaux). Talk to your lawyer and then send in an investigator to interview everybody under attorney-client privilege. Get the story nailed down while you still have the chance.

If you think a lawsuit could come from an employee, prepare accordingly. If you have a member of your team who is persistently negative, for instance, you should nip that in the bud. Talk to them about their negativity; if nothing changes, it's time for them to move on. As we've emphasized, building a winning team is sometimes a matter of weeding out certain employees and then upgrading your staff by adding someone with greater skills and a better attitude. Of course, since this is the chapter on legal protection, we should also note that you should carefully document your reasons for terminating someone. If it's a particularly sticky situation, consider bringing in an employment lawyer or a consultant to get statements from your staff. Remember that people will say different things while they're still waiting to get their last paycheck than they will several months down the road. For more information on how to safely terminate an employee, make sure you or your practice manager watch the training video Alan created on the subject. You can access this video for free at **www.GrowMyMedicalPractice.com**.

The Thundering Importance of Umbrella Coverage

A $5 million umbrella liability policy is usually quite affordable, and it can make all the difference if you find yourself suddenly caught in a legal storm. If you don't have at least a $2 million policy—or ideally, a $5 million policy—consider taking care of that right away.

Common-Sense Tips for Reducing the Odds You'll Ever Be Sued

There are some fairly simple things you can do in your day-to-day practice to dramatically reduce the risk of ever being sued in the first place. Try the following on for size.

Be likable. You should regard being likable as part of your job. When Dr. Challa takes the time to ask each patient about something that's personally important to him or her, he's not doing it to avoid getting sued— but it sure helps. At Alan's law practice, he regularly sees this issue from the other side when he meets with a family dealing with the estate of a deceased loved one. "We think the doctor made a mistake," they'll often say, "but we really like him. We're not suing." Likability is a key part of the psychology of medical lawsuits.

What does it take to make a patient like you? Dr. Challa's approach is a great one; if possible, make notes about personal details and remember to ask about those things in follow-up visits. Also, remember that very small gestures and learnable behaviors can make an enormous difference. Say the patient's name when you greet them. Make eye contact in which you see the color of their eyes and remember it. If appropriate, continue to make eye contact throughout the appointment. Ideally, sit down when you're talking with them so that you're at eye level. This will feel to them like you're really spending time on their exam, as compared to how they'd feel if you remained standing throughout their entire appointment. Then, at the end of the appointment, touch them on the shoulder or knee, and say their name again as you say good-bye. These behaviors might sound insignificant, but they make an incredible difference to the patient.

It's also important to apologize if you were late or your office made an error. If necessary, consider having a nurse go out to the waiting room and explain that you were caught up in an emergency and you're now running behind schedule. "We're very sorry," the nurse should say to the assembled patients, "and we'll be glad to reschedule your appointment if you'd prefer that." Similarly, if you enter the exam room behind schedule, just a few words will make all the difference: "I'm so sorry I'm late. Now, Maureen, how are you today?"

It's also important to be likable when it comes to your staff. Physicians who are not well liked by their team, hospital nursing, or other employees may have a bright-red bull's-eye on their back. Those who are well liked may be saved from disaster time and again. Simple courtesy and kindness can mean the difference between good times and disaster. If you lose your temper or are abrupt, apologize immediately.

Follow the thirty-second rule. This is a relatively simple safeguard that can make a big difference. When you're in the exam room with a patient, or afterward when you're dictating notes, take thirty seconds to consider how this patient could sue you. What's the most likely thing to go wrong? Then act accordingly. If she's taking a medication and it's imperative that she take the entire bottle, emphasize that when you're in the exam room, and then put it in your notes: "Told her to take entire bottle." (Ideally, have a nurse make a follow-up call to ensure that she is indeed taking the whole bottle.) You get the idea.

Don't stand alone with high-risk patients. Don't rely solely on your own malpractice insurance to protect you. It's generally not too expensive to get a $1 million policy for a mid-level provider. Then, when you find yourself in the exam room with a high-risk patient, bring that mid-level into the room with you; that way, her policy will be in play as well. As an additional safeguard, send the high-risk patient to another specialist for a second opinion, thereby also bringing that provider's insurance into play. What you don't want to do is stand alone with a standard $250,000/$750,000 policy. We'll say it one final time: Don't stand alone when the risk is high.

Legal Guidance Is Not One-Size-Fits-All

Though it's a good start, the above guidance is not meant to be comprehensive. Remember, all legal guidance is not created equal. Just because you've done some asset protection doesn't mean it's sufficient or that it has been done properly. In these complex issues, mistakes are common. Enlist an attorney who specializes in serving medical practices.

The time to protect yourself is now. Plenty of doctors try to transfer assets into protected vehicles only after a lawsuit has been initiated. That won't work. The court will consider it a fraudulent transfer and set the money aside. So don't delay!

Of course, we understand that legal protection isn't your favorite subject. But there may come a day when you'll thank us, especially Alan, for covering such a heavy subject. With that behind us, we've now tackled five crucial ways of accelerating your practice, from strengthening your core and engaging your team to cultivating your culture, enhancing your profitability, and covering your backside. Now it's time for the sixth and final accelerator.

CHAPTER 10

Accelerator Six:
Hire a Coach

After six months of working with a coach, Dr. Landon (the surgeon you first read about back in Chapter 1) began to see profound differences at his practice. The biggest change, and the easiest to quantify, was the uptick in profitability associated with the changes he'd made to his medical spa, which we described in Chapter 8. With the right financial insight and support, he had turned a $100,000-a-year loss into a $150,000-a-year profit center.

Yet that change was just the beginning of the positive benefits that came from Dr. Landon's new coaching support. "It's been significant in so many different ways," he recently told us, after seeing more than a year of positive results.

A crucial improvement came from the administrative support that he now has access to, thanks to the contacts he made through Maui Mastermind, David's coaching practice.

"We had very poor accounting in the office," Dr. Landon acknowledges. "It was through the people we met at the Maui meetings that we got involved with an accounting group that almost exclusively deals with medical practices." This change has helped put him on top of his financials.

He also saw benefits from a legal perspective—something that you know a great deal about after reading the last chapter. "We thought we were asset protected. We had spent huge amounts of money establishing LLCs, only to find out that we were probably just about as exposed as we could be," he told us. He has since taken the necessary precautions to get his practice protected.

What's more, Dr. Landon and his practice manager now have access to an expert who serves as a regular sounding board. "As things arise week to week, we never really had anybody from a business standpoint whom we could bounce ideas off of. Now we can drop an email to say, 'This has come up. What are your thoughts?' It's instant advice that we never had."

Perhaps the most significant change of all has been Dr. Landon's upgraded approach to his own role as manager. Whereas he used to tend to management-related responsibilities as an afterthought, he now firmly believes in dedicating prime blocks of time each week to the important work of managing his practice and steering it toward a prosperous future.

Though he acknowledges that he might have figured this stuff out on his own eventually, Dr. Landon says that by seeking help from a professional coach, he dramatically shortened his learning curve, reducing mistakes and stumbles along the way.

"There's always that notion that it's too expensive a luxury to have a business coach," says Dr. Landon, "but what we've seen is that the money to pay for the coaching program many times over was already there in our practice, and our coach just helped us see and execute on the changes to unlock it. In just the first twelve months of coaching, we've reaped a staggering return on investment on our coaching. Best of all, I'm actually working five to ten hours *less* each week. You can't put a price on that.

"I've seen what a difference working on my practice in a structured way has made for me personally," he adds. "The practice runs more smoothly, it's more profitable, and our staff is happier. Stop making excuses and take that first step."

Enlist a Coach to Hold You Accountable and Accelerate Your Progress

A coach is an experienced entrepreneur who has been where you want to go and can give you the outside perspective and counsel you need to build a more successful practice—so you don't have to go through all the painful trial and error yourself. Just as a coach does for a sports team, a business coach's role is to help you focus, plan, execute, and regroup, so that you make consistent progress growing your practice and making it owner independent.

A coach can serve another function as well: to be the one person in your professional life who will tell you the things you don't want to hear but desperately *need* to hear. Too many doctors build their practices in isolation, lacking the outside perspective and feedback of an experienced mentor. What's more, most doctors don't have anyone in their network who actively challenges their thinking or questions their assumptions. Sure, you may have lots of employees, but these people depend on you for their families' financial support, and to ask someone in that position to challenge you is asking a lot.

David's friend and coauthor of *SCALE*, Jeff Hoffman (the cofounder of Priceline.com), put it this way: "What I get out of having a business coach is that my coach has run and worked with so many companies that he's seen almost every situation. So when I don't know how to handle a new situation, my coach says, 'Don't worry about it. I've seen this pattern a dozen times. Here's how best to handle it.'"

Our Top Tips for Getting the Most Out of Your Coach

- **Pick a coach who has a deep base of experience and knowledge** to draw upon. The whole idea of leveraging a coach is to help you avoid a lot of the expensive trial and error from which most doctors suffer as they build their practices. While many of the situations you come up against in your practice may be new to you, your coach can draw on his past experiences to give you clarity on the best path forward.

- **Pick a coach who can articulate and explain things to you in simple, step-by-step language** so that you can integrate what the coach shares and put it to immediate and effective use.

- **Meet frequently with your coach—but not *too* often.** We recommend every two weeks as the optimal interval. This is often enough that you get effective accountability (monthly is generally not often enough), but not so often that you don't have time to get things done.

- **Give your coach weekly** updates on your progress. Taking five to fifteen minutes each week to update your coach on your progress adds a layer of accountability *and* keeps your coach up to speed with your practice so she can give you her best input. David's business-coaching clients use his company's "Big Rock App" each week to automatically update their coach on their progress from the prior week.

- **Share your numbers—candidly.** Yes, it can be scary to share your revenue, gross margin, and operating-profit figures with complete candor, but by being open you will get valuable outside perspective and feedback (remember how important this was for Dr. Landon!).

Don't sugarcoat anything. Your coach won't judge you. His goal is to help you grow and succeed, and to do that, he needs accurate data.

- **Don't just focus on one-off challenges; look for systematic, global solutions.** Solving a challenge is great, but solving a challenge in a way that improves and develops your practice's internal systems and controls is even more valuable. Ad hoc solutions are hard to scale. Systems-driven solutions are more stable and easier to grow.

- **Pick a program, not just a coach.** You want and need more than just a great coach; you want a solid, proven coaching *program*. Remember, structure plus talent always outperforms talent on its own. In effect, the right coaching program makes sure that your coach balances your practice's immediate day-to-day operational needs with its longer-term development strategy.

A Big Impact—Not Just for Dr. Challa, but for His Staff as Well

By the time Dr. Challa sought coaching services from David's practice, the Kansas Medical Clinic was a relatively mature organization.

"We were so mature we didn't think we needed any coaching," says Dr. Challa. "Wrong. David has no problem telling me, 'Hey, slow down. Hey, don't do it this way,' because he's my coach. My downstream staff might not have the guts to say that to me."

Dr. Challa and his COO, Michelle, now meet with David on a regular basis, which has yielded enormous results. Indeed, in many cases, it makes sense to enlist coaching guidance not only for the organizational leader, but also for key staff members. Dr. Challa and Michelle work together with David, building and executing their quarterly Action Plan and ironing out organizational problems together.

Dr. Challa has also seen great benefits from sending key staff members to David's conferences.

"Depending on the conference," Dr. Challa says, "we pick and choose whom we send. If it's operational issues, then Michelle or I may go. If it's marketing, we send our marketing people. This doesn't just increase their knowledge base as they get better at what they're doing; what we are indirectly telling them by sending them is that we're investing in their growth. That goes a long way. It increases their passion. From their perspective, it becomes clear that we care about them."

- **Give your coach permission to hold you accountable.** The right coach will always be in your corner, and sometimes this means being the one person in your business life who calls you to the mat. Your employees can't do this because you sign their paychecks.

- **Don't rationalize or explain away reality,** because even if you win the discussion, reality will still win the war. We smile when we think about all the exceptionally smart and articulate doctors we've known over the years who at one point or another thought they could explain away a problem with a good argument. Reality is what reality is, and the objective facts are the objective facts. Your coach will help you cut through your own rationalizations, helping you take full responsibility and accept the facts on the ground. And from this place, you can work together to come up with an effective Action Plan to harness those facts to reach your goals.

- **Let go of your ego** and accept the help and insights of your coach. In this relationship, you don't have to posture or look good. Your coach has seen just about everything you're dealing with and has worked through it. Let your coach save you time, energy, emotion, and money by helping you learn from her experiences rather than taking the painful and expensive route of trial and error.

- **Get rid of your excuses.** You don't have to do it perfectly, but you do have to take action. Of course you're busy, but when will that ever really change if you don't do the things that will reduce your practice's reliance on you? If you want to enjoy the growth and freedom that the right coach can help you achieve, then you've got to let go of your excuses and dive fully into the commitment. Sure, you'll mess up and have setbacks, but we've seen the magic that can happen over thirty-six months (or more) of focused, directed, intelligent action in scaling a practice. The time will pass either way. What will you be saying three years from today? "If only I had . . ." or "I'm so glad . . ."? Dive in, and put your coach's guidance into action.

Every top athlete has an experienced coach, and so do many of the world's most successful entrepreneurs. Your coach's job is to help push you to perform at your best and avoid the costly mistakes that plague most doctors as they build their practices.

It's hard for you to gain the perspective you need to see your practice with the necessary clarity. This is what the right coach will do for you. He or she will push you, challenge you, support you, and guide you. The right coach will hold you accountable in a structured, programmatic way. It's our experience that the right coaching program balances your practice's

Scale Your Mission, Earn More, and Work Less

Bonnie J. Hacker is the founder of Emerge—A Child's Place, a therapeutic practice in North Carolina that is focused on the care of children. Bonnie was a gifted clinician who directly helped hundreds of families, personally assisting children in dealing with developmental and behavioral challenges.

When Bonnie first started working with her coach, she was struggling with the loss of her longtime practice manager, Karen. When Karen left, Bonnie initially panicked. So much of the administrative, billing, and operational systems were just informally stored in Karen's head, and now she was leaving. But working with her coach, Bonnie quickly recovered. She hired an upgraded office manager to replace Karen. And this time, she followed the structured methodology to grow her practice that you've learned about in this book. Every quarter, she and David's team cocreated her one-page quarterly Action Plan. She dutifully met with her coach every two weeks to gain outside perspective and accountability so that she consistently executed on her plan to grow her practice and reduce its reliance on her. The outcome?

"Here I am six years after diligently applying these strategies to build an owner-independent practice. I've reduced my working hours to under ten a week, and the practice continues to serve the children we see exceptionally well. At the same time, we've grown our revenues by 145 percent."

immediate day-to-day needs with crucial longer-term strategy. If your coach just helps you deal with your current challenges but doesn't give you a clear map to consistently reduce your company's reliance on you by enhancing its systems, team, controls, and culture, you just may end up more firmly trapped in an owner-reliant Level Two business.

In fact, we'll go one better. If building an owner-independent Level Three company isn't a stated goal and structural objective of the coaching program you are considering, don't join. Find a program that has the right mix of coaching magic and program structure and experience to accelerate you to Level Three.

Five Steps to Enhance Your Practice *Right* Now

ongratulations! You've made it to the final chapter—a huge accomplishment. You've not only invested the time to read the rich array of practice-building strategies and concepts we've shared, but also, and more importantly, you've embraced the vision of building an owner-independent Level Three practice.

Now it's time for you to step up and apply what you've learned. In this final chapter, you'll find five simple steps you can take immediately to accelerate your progress to Level Three. Before we get to those action steps, though, let's take a second to consider the potential payoff. Specifically, consider how this methodical approach worked for Dr. Park.

Dr. Park runs a highly successful pain-management clinic in Florida. When he looks back on his career, he sees a crucial transformation that took place when he made a very important decision. Here's how he describes it:

"Most doctors are burned out because they're trying to practice medicine full-time and they're trying to manage their practices full-time, *and* that doesn't work. At some point, you have to make a decision: Am I going to continue to practice medicine and hire a practice administrator? Or am I going to become a practice manager and hire a doctor to replace me? That's where most doctors get stuck. I understand this because I reached that point myself."

When he reached this crossroads, Dr. Park did a bit of soul-searching.

"We had a lot of other services that we could have offered. We had a lot of other growth opportunities. I was passionate about what I was doing, and I was making a lot of money—but it got to the point where it just wasn't sustainable."

He started to think carefully about the future. He pictured himself down the road, wanting to cut down on his hours and eventually retire. Yet he knew that when he got to that point, he would *also* want to maintain ownership of his practice in order to generate an income even when he was no longer present. What's more, he aspired not only to maintain ownership of the practice, but also to own the building and surgery center that housed it. That way, after he retired, he would draw an income not only through his share of medical revenue, but also through rent. With this vision in mind, Dr. Park set about making his goals a reality.

It wasn't a quick process, but it was a very successful one. He did it piece by piece: He invested in real estate, and he invested, one team member at a time, in a world-class staff, all the while keeping in mind the objective of building a pain-management clinic that would eventually run without his daily involvement.

Today, Dr. Park employs not one, not two, but *three* managers at his practice, all of whom oversee different areas, including the core medical practice, the ambulatory surgery center, and billing and HR.

"My three managers do most of the heavy lifting," he told us recently, "and I coordinate their efforts and consult with them. I give them my opinion and let them fly. If they get good outcomes, great. If they don't, then we learn from the experience, and go from there."

Dr. Park's practice is a great success. But perhaps the greatest success is the way it has enabled him to live precisely the life he wants. He now spends six months out of every year in Hawaii, where he loves to surf (and, yes, you read that right: *six months out of every year*). He and his significant other play tennis every single day, year round. And when we last spoke with him, he hadn't seen patients in an entire year—even as his practice hums and continues to grow.

If you're ready to build the practice that you envision, and to transform your own life along with it, then it's time to take the following five action steps to push yourself toward your goal.

Five Simple Steps to Get Started Now

Action Step #1: Make building an owner-independent Level Three practice a stated goal for yourself and your practice.

On May 25, 1961, in a speech before a joint session of Congress, President John F. Kennedy set out a bold goal: "I believe that this nation should commit itself to achieving the goal, before this decade is out, of landing a man on the moon and returning him safely to the earth." This commitment galvanized the United States in a decade-long race that famously culminated on July 20, 1969, with Neil Armstrong and Buzz Aldrin landing on the moon.

Are we saying that the goal of building an owner-independent practice is the business equivalent of a moon shot? Far from it. But our combined seventy-one years of working in, on, or with medical practices has taught us to respect and harness the power of a clearly articulated and shared vision. That's why we're emphasizing that your first step after putting this book down is to make building an owner-independent Level Three practice a stated goal.

When your team members understand that this is important for their future—both for increased job security and for greater opportunities to contribute and earn—they will gradually buy into this shared vision.

This isn't an overnight change, of course, but a longer-term commitment. Consider your personal reasons for wanting to build an owner-independent practice. Whose lives will your practice touch by holding true to your Level Three vision? How will owning a Level Three practice affect your family? Your employees? Your community? How will it allow you to give more money and time to causes you care deeply about? How will you be an inspiration to others? We grow wealthy by what we give; how will you share your good fortune on a bigger playing field? Remember, you can never really pay it back, but you can pay it forward.

You should also enlist the help of each of your team members, asking them to articulate their own deeper reasons for being part of this journey with your practice. How does building a Level Three practice support *their* life goals? When you're all working toward one common goal, you will marvel at the heights you can reach.

Action Step #2: Reclaim some of your best time by taking a Focus Day each week.

Start small and build from there. While you can't control your entire week, you can reclaim *at least two hours one day each week* as your Focus Day. If you're able, make this a four-hour block, but at the very least, claim two hours every week to focus on the A- and B-level activities that really create value for your practice.

Put this block on your calendar as an appointment. You wouldn't be so rude as to stand up someone with whom you had a meeting, so treat your Focus Day with the same degree of respect. Don't stand yourself up—or your practice.

Once you show up for this appointment, don't use this valuable time for routine activities like catching up on email messages or dictating notes. Remember, this block of time is the raw ingredient you need to engage in the high-leverage activities that will push your practice forward. This is time set aside to step out of the role of medical provider and into the role of practice leader and value creator.

We believe that once you see the cumulative power of these precious blocks of time, you'll become hooked and follow our other time-mastery suggestions, including scheduling a one-hour Prime-Time block on each Push Day. But at the very least, we know you can take a two-hour Focus Day each week, and this will serve as the starting point for truly advancing your practice.

Dr. Singh has gotten to the point where he dedicates every Tuesday and Thursday to A- and B-level activities. Dr. Challa's Focus Day is every Wednesday afternoon. Now it's your turn. Make a commitment, and write it down.

My Focus Day is: _____.

Action Step #3: Conduct your Sweet Spot analysis.

Back in Chapter 3, as part of developing your one-page Action Plan, we described a process for identifying what we call your practice's "Sweet Spots." Now it's time to conduct that analysis. Ask yourself this: What is the single biggest limiting factor at your practice? In other words, what one limitation is currently doing the most to constrain the growth and success of your practice? Many physicians realize, for instance, that provider capacity is their single biggest constraint. For others, it's patient volume; they need more patients coming in the door. For others, the limitation is space. And so on. As of today, what is your practice's single biggest limiting factor?

Now brainstorm ten or more ways to address this limiting factor (that's right, *a minimum of ten* solutions). So let's say your problem is patient volume. Possible solutions include starting a Friends and Family referral program, implementing a reactivation strategy, and hiring an outside contracting company to do social media advertising. Or, if your constraint is your physical location, you might consider talking with the person next door about subleasing some of their space, or looking for a satellite location, or taking telemedicine appointments, or staggering business hours. You get the idea.

Once you have your list of ten or more ideas, now it's time to apply the two filters that you learned about in Chapter 3: You're looking for the Low-Hanging Fruit and the Home Runs. Low-Hanging Fruit are solutions that are easy or straightforward to implement, and that are highly likely to work and produce results. A Home Run is a solution whose payoff is significant if it works. On your list of solutions, circle the Low-Hanging Fruit and the Home Runs. Which items are both Low-Hanging Fruit and Home Runs? These are your Sweet Spots—the solutions that deserve a solid investment of your time, attention, *and* money, because you'll reap an exponential return.

Keep in mind that the Sweet Spot analysis isn't something you should do only once. In order to achieve steady growth at your practice, you need to repeat this analysis every quarter. Pause and ask yourself, "What's our number-one limiting factor right now?" It's going to change over time—and it *should* change over time. Overcoming one constraint will expose another, and so on. Continue to conduct your Sweet Spot analysis to keep on growing.

Action Step #4: Register for your free practice-building tool kit.

Want to access any of the tools we've shared in the pages of this book? Looking for a way to help your staff access powerful practice-building training videos? We've spent hundreds of hours and tens of thousands of dollars putting together this practice-building tool kit. And it is our free gift to you.

Yes, you heard us right: It's a free gift for you and your staff. Consider it our way of making a deeper investment in you. The tool kit includes dozens of online training videos, downloadable PDF tools, and links to some of the best practice-growth resources available on the web.

We believe you were born to make a difference in your community, and we want to concretely support you on your journey to building a Level Three medical practice. To gain immediate access to this powerful tool kit, go to **www.GrowMyMedicalPractice.com**. (See Appendix A for full details.)

Action Step #5: Try out a free business-coaching session.

If you're intrigued with the idea of getting expert, outside perspective and the structured support and accountability to rapidly accelerate your practice's success, then talk with a business coach.

In fact, we believe so strongly in the value of coaching to help you grow your practice the right way that we've arranged for you to get a complimentary coaching session with one of David's senior business coaches. Let's be clear, we're talking about a real, working session on your practice and the best path to reaching your business and financial goals.

We'll conduct this private, one-on-one, ninety-minute coaching session by phone or web conference. We've learned that this is the best way—by actually doing a real coaching session—for you to determine if coaching is right for you. You'll gain a greater sense of clarity about the best strategies and path to growing your medical practice. To check on availability and schedule your complimentary coaching session, just visit **www.GrowMyMedicalPractice.com/freecoachingsession**.

You Can Do It—and the Rewards Are Well Worth It

Dr. Park's success is a powerful example of how the strategies in this book can transform your practice and your personal life. But we'd like to leave you with one final story about why it's so profoundly important to make your practice owner independent. Consider, in particular, what happened to Dr. Tom Umbach and his wife, Holly.

Dr. Umbach is a bariatric surgeon in Nevada. When he first started working with David's coaching practice, he was putting in eight to ten hours a day of surgery and patient consults and then doing practice management in the evenings or on weekends. At the same time, his wife, Holly, was working as his practice manager—though, truth be told, she didn't really *want* to be office manager. But they were stuck. They didn't have the right systems or controls in place to hire anyone else.

"Looking back at my ten years of training to become a surgeon, I received an excellent medical education, but almost no training in how to be a businessperson running a medical practice," Dr. Umbach says now. That realization led him to seek assistance from David's coaching practice.

With the guidance of a coach, Dr. Umbach and Holly both committed themselves to growing the practice to Level Three. They diligently began doing the work to put in place the right systems and hire the right people.

Dr. Umbach describes the change in his thinking during this time: "Do you continue to see yourself as the sole producer in your medical practice, or are you willing to promote other producers? That's a big mental hurdle. It took me a long time to get that."

Holly also had to learn to let go of her control of the practice.

"When you're growing a business, it's your baby," she explains. "It's a really huge hurdle to jump, to let go and feel comfortable that somebody is going to catch you on the other side. You're relying on other people to do their jobs."

Despite these hurdles, they made remarkable progress toward growing their surgery practice to Level Three.

And it was a good thing they did.

Not long ago, Holly was diagnosed with breast cancer. Suddenly the Umbachs were confronting a life-threatening illness. Of course, Holly had to step away from her responsibilities at the practice, but there were also times when Dr. Umbach needed to excuse himself, and at a moment's notice.

If they had not done the collaborative work of maturing their practice, Holly's cancer would not only have been the horrendous personal event that it was; it also would have been a disaster for the practice.

Instead, because they had the right systems, team members, and practice culture in place, it presented no challenge at all. In fact, Holly describes it as "a walk in the park, from a business perspective." Since they had another surgeon who could pick up some of Dr. Umbach's cases, Holly says, "we didn't lose any revenue when he had to step away for a day or two to help me through the cancer."

What if they had not done all that work to radically reduce the practice's reliance on Dr. Umbach? "Had we still been at Level One, obviously, it would have been a huge business fiasco," Dr. Umbach told us.

Today, we're happy to report that Holly is healthy—and so is Dr. Umbach's surgery practice. Both are so healthy, in fact, that Holly and Dr. Umbach recently took a vacation to Mexico. "That was really the first time that Tom stopped taking business calls," Holly told us. "It's the first time that I've seen him actually stop and sit—in seventeen years!"

"It was really nice, I've got to say," Dr. Umbach chimed in. "I was able to read some books I'd been meaning to read for a while, and not have to think about the practice. I could really get away from the practice and recharge with Holly."

If you were to ask Dr. Umbach if he ever thought, at the start of his Level Three journey, that he would succeed the way he has, he would tell you that he struggled with the same doubts and fears that you do. Remember that feeling afraid is normal when you're stretching yourself and going after your dreams. It's a sign that you're growing.

If you ever doubt your capacity to stay the course and reach Level Three, then borrow our faith. We know you can do it. And you're not alone; this is a journey that thousands of other physicians in our physician community are taking with you. Together, we can support one another and accomplish our goals.

The three of us have seen the impact of following the ideas and coaching suggestions we've laid out for you in the pages of this book. Now is your time.

Thank you for letting us guide you in building an owner-independent practice. Enjoy your journey to Level Three; it is worth the investment of time, energy, and money to build a practice you love owning, and to get your life back.

About the Authors

David Finkel is a former Olympic-level athlete turned business multimillionaire, and is one of the nation's most respected business thinkers. He is a *Wall Street Journal* and *BusinessWeek* best-selling author of twelve business books, including *SCALE: 7 Proven Principles to Grow Your Business* and *Get Your Life Back*, which he coauthored with Priceline.com cofounder Jeff Hoffman.

David is the founder and CEO of Maui Mastermind® (**www.MauiMastermind.com** and **www.GrowMyMedicalPractice.com**), one of the world's premier business-coaching companies, which has worked with hundreds of medical groups and physicians to help them grow their practices and get their lives back. David's business-coaching clients enjoy an average annual growth rate that is five times higher than that of the average privately held company in the United States, while at the same time increasing their companies' owner independence by an average of 87.4 percent. Over the past twenty years, David and the other Maui coaches and advisors have personally scaled companies with an aggregate market value of $63 billion.

His weekly business-owner e-letter is read by 100,000 business owners around the world, and his syndicated business articles on Inc.com and Huffingtonpost.com garner over 250,000 readers every year. His work has been featured in such prestigious media outlets as the *Wall Street Journal*, *International Business Times*, *Bloomberg Businessweek*, *Fast Company*, *Fox Business*, *MSNBC*, and *Inc.* magazine.

An in-demand keynote speaker, David's message of how to grow a business by strengthening its core systems, team, and culture has galvanized business audiences around the globe.

He and his wife, Heather, and their three sons live in Jackson Hole, Wyoming.

Pariksith Singh, MD, is board certified in internal medicine. He received his medical education at Sawai Man Singh Medical College in Rajasthan, India, where he was awarded honors in internal medicine and physiology. Dr. Singh completed a residency in internal medicine at Mount Sinai Elmhurst Services in New York.

Dr. Singh founded Access Health Care LLC (**www.ahcpllc.com**) as a single-location clinic in 2001. Today Access Health Care is a $164-million medical company with 83 offices serving 66,000 patients. They employ a staff of 900, including 177 physicians and providers.

Dr. Singh was also the founder and CEO of Optimum HealthCare, Inc., which later merged with Freedom HMO to form one of the largest Medicare HMOs in the country, with total revenues of over $1 billion annually. He also founded Integral Healthcare, LLC, which is one of the most profitable ACOs per patient in the United States.

Dr. Singh dedicates much of his time to philanthropic endeavors, for which he was awarded the Frist Humanitarian Award. He is passionate about supporting the Wounded Warrior Project in Hernando County.

Dr. Singh and his wife, Dr. Scunziano, have four active children, who certainly keep them on their toes! In addition to family activities, Dr. Singh's hobbies include writing poetry, and studying literature, religion, and philosophy. He and his family live in Spring Hill, Florida.

Alan Gassman, JD, LL.M, is senior partner with Gassman, Crotty, & Denicolo, PA. AV® Pre-eminent™ Peer Review Rated by Martindale-Hubbard®, Alan has been on the board of advisors of the Journal of Asset Protection, a fellow in the American Bar Association National Association of Estate Planners & Councils, and a member of the Florida Bar since 1994.

As one of the nation's top physicians' attorneys, Alan has been serving physicians and medical groups for over thirty years. His deep knowledge and experience working with the specialized needs of doctors led him to become one of the most sought after speakers and medical attorneys in the country.

Alan is a Board Certified Wills, Trusts and Estates Lawyer by the Florida Board of Legal Specialization Accredited Estate Planner, National Association of Estate Planners & Councils. Alan has authored more than 200 articles and law school textbook contributions.

Alan and his wife, Marcia, live in Clearwater, Florida.

His firm can be reached at (727) 442-1200 or online at **www.gassmanlaw.com**.

Acknowledgments

We want to thank the people who made a huge difference in the creation of this book and the online tools at **www.GrowMyMedical Practice.com**.

First, we collectively want to thank Mattea, Michael, and their editorial team, who are such skilled wordsmiths and an absolute pleasure to work with.

Next, we want to thank all the physicians who agreed to let us share their story in this book. While we have changed a few identifying details at the request of some of them, all the physicians you have read about in the pages of this book are practicing physicians who have made it their life's work to care for their patients.

David's Thanks:
Thank you, Alan and Pariksith. You are both extraordinary at what you do and were a pleasure to work with on this project. Alan, thanks for being my attorney and always taking my call when I'm in need of objective perspective. To my team at Maui Mastermind, thank you for your full buy-in to our mission of helping business owners grow their companies and get their lives back. You are a joy to work with and have my utmost respect and gratitude. Finally, to the many business-coaching clients of ours who generously shared your stories for this book, thank you. You are making a real difference for other medical groups around the country through your example.

Pariksith's Thanks:
My sincerest gratitude to my patients, who are are my best teachers. They keep me grounded while inspiring me to newer heights. I also thank my parents, who have now become my friends. I thank my team and coworkers, who know far more than I do. I thank my wife, Dr. Maria Scunziano, and our four children. And, of course, my thanks to Alan and David.

Alan's Thanks:
It would take pages to properly thank all of the people who have made this book and its contents possible. First, to David, who is an amazing coach, mentor, and friend. My time associated with Maui Mastermind and its wonderful community has been a game changer in many ways. To Pariksith, who is a tremendous inspiration. You are living proof that business science can be coupled with medical practices for the good of all concerned. My most important contribution to this book was introducing David and Pariksith. I thank our team of lawyers and legal assistants, who share my quest to be the best that we can be in order to best serve our physician clients, and I thank my wife, Marcia, for keeping me balanced in the process. Finally, thank you to the hundreds of physicians that we have had the honor to represent in all manners of law and life for over thirty years. What you do for patients, your teams, and our society is as valuable as life itself, and not well recognized or appreciated by so many who take what you do for granted. I hope that this book provides solid best steps and strategies to make your professional life better than you thought was possible, like so many of David's clients and Pariksith's followers have been doing for years.

Finally, we want to jointly thank you, the reader, for investing the time to read this book. We wish you every success in your journey.

The Medical Practice Success Tool Kit: Your <u>FREE</u> $1,375 Gift from the Authors

Dear Reader,

As our way of supporting your mission to grow your medical practice and serve more patients, and to do so in a way that gives you more time and freedom, we've created a unique online tool kit to help you and your key staff apply the ideas you've learned in this book.

To register, all you need to do is go to **www.GrowMyMedical Practice.com**, and you'll gain immediate access to this powerful collection of practice growth tools. They're designed to help physicians like you apply the ideas in this book to grow your practice and get your life back.

The Medical Practice Success Tool Kit includes over a dozen video-training modules to help you grow your practice according to proven best practices. Designed for physicians, practice managers, and your support staff, these training videos will help you increase your patient volume, recruit and intelligently onboard new providers, and control your practice expenses.

You'll also be able to download the PDF tools included in this book, and a few that we didn't have room for but which David uses with his business-coaching clients.

Finally, you'll receive regular updates, articles, and ongoing invitations to web-based trainings that you and your key staff can leverage to improve your practice.

Here are just a few of the training videos you'll see:

- How to Apply the 6 Practice Accelerators to Reach Your Practice Goals Faster
- How to Strengthen Your "Practice Core" to Increase Efficiencies, Improve Profitability, and Better Serve Your Patients
- 21 Cash-Flow Secrets to Help Your Practice Earn More
- 12 Asset-Protection Strategies Every Physician Must Know to Reduce Their Personal and Practice Exposures
- The 10 Biggest Scaling Mistakes Medical Practices Make (and How You Can Avoid Making Them)

And much more . . .

We've even added an entire section on the key legal issues you face, based on Alan's extensive work as one of the nation's leading physician attorneys. You'll gain clear insights into how best to structure your employment agreements and non-competes, hospital integrations, and other critical areas of practice law. This one section alone will give you greater peace of mind and clarity on how you must operate your practice to reduce your liability and enhance your success.

Limited-Time Extra Bonus:
Free, Private 90-Minute Business Coaching Session

For a limited time, you'll get one more bonus from the Medical Practice Success Tool Kit: a confidential 90-minute practice Growth Strategy Session with one of David's senior business coaches.

This deep-dive strategy session will help you pinpoint the key constraints to growing your practice and map out the best ways to grow. Think of this as your way to get our concrete assistance in applying the concepts and strategies you've been reading about in this book to your specific practice and personal circumstances.

Register Now to Get Immediate Access to This Free Bonus

Simply go to **www.GrowMyMedicalPractice.com** and register right now. It's that easy, and you'll gain immediate access to this invaluable tool kit for your practice.

Again, we thank you for reading this book. We wish you every success in growing your practice.

Sincerely,

David, Pariksith, and Alan

P.S. Because this free tool kit is a limited-time offer and may be changed or pulled at any time, we strongly encourage you to go to **www.GrowMyMedicalPractice.com** and register *now*.

Get Your Life Back Faster

Dear Reader,

Most physicians who own and operate a private practice want growth, but they hold themselves back because they fear that to get that growth, they'll have to sacrifice their lives. As you've learned in the pages of this book, the only way to *sustainably* grow your practice is to reduce its reliance on you. Done right, you get growth *and* you get your life back.

For over a decade now, we've helped thousands of physicians just like you build thriving owner-independent practices. And I want to invite you to explore the possibility of our working together to help you grow your medical practice the right way.

I do want to caution you: If you're looking for a magic bullet, the Business Coaching Program is not for you. It's for serious business owners who want to legitimately break through to the next level and build a thriving, owner-independent medical practice.

Imagine tapping into this proven program. No more guessing, no more struggling, no more doubting yourself or your decisions. Just consistent growth and greater time freedom.

For years, this is exactly what we've been doing: helping physicians like you run their practices more smoothly and profitably, by giving them the business insights, best practices, and structure that they never learned about in medical school.

And we'll help you do all this by working *fewer hours*. The program is designed to leverage the skills, talent, and commitment of your current staff to do much of the heavy lifting for you, so that this becomes an immediately doable process of growth.

How can we be so confident that we can help you get great results? That's a fair question. And my answer is simple: We've been successfully doing exactly that for a long time.

In the pages of this book, we have already introduced you to many of our successful clients. You've learned about the dramatic difference that working together has had on their practices and their lives. What they all have in common is that they've recognized that being part of a *structured*, proven program is the fastest and surest way to succeed. And now it's your turn.

If you're serious about building an owner-independent practice and want outside, expert guidance to do it in the best way possible, I urge you to go online and schedule a confidential 90-minute Practice Growth Strategy Session with one of our senior business coaches. Just go to **www.GrowMyMedicalPractice.com/freecoachingsession** to schedule your session now.

This private, one-on-one call is an actual *working session*. We'll do a deep dive into your practice and map out the best way to grow it. In fact, we'll do this session as if you were already one of our business coaching clients, so that you can get a real sense of what it would be like to work with us, and we can get a real feel for what it would be like to work with you as a client if we invited you into the program.

There is no cost or obligation on either side. Past experience has shown us that this is the most accurate way to try out the fit on both sides.

Regardless of whether you're interested in ongoing coaching support, you'll leave the session with a greater sense of clarity about the best strategy for growing your medical practice, including the top leverage points and concrete action steps to take.

Don't miss out on this opportunity. The Business Coaching Program was designed to give you the structure *and* the accountability, the map *and* the upgraded peer group, the direction *and* the feedback that you need to take your business to the next level.

You don't have to go it alone. Together, we will make certain that you'll succeed, and that you'll succeed faster, with less trial and error than you ever could have otherwise.

Sincerely,

David Finkel
CEO
Maui Mastermind

P.S. Stop building your practice in isolation and let our experienced team coach and guide you. **Go to <u>www.GrowMyMedicalPractice.com/free coachingsession</u> or call us toll-free at 1-844-584-4000 right now.**

Decision-making:
  strategic, 11, 29
  top-down vs. bottom-up, 66–68, 69
Defined benefit plans, 94
Digital folders, 45–48
Discipline, 23–25
Distractions, 24–25
Drug reps, 85

Efficiency, 44, 46, 58
"80 Percent Mass," 15
80/20 Rule, 14, 16, 92
Emerge—A Child's Place, 106
Employed physicians, 6, 60–62
Employees. *See* Team members
EMR codes, 86
Encouragement, 72
Environment, 23–25
Estate planning, 94
Expense controls, 83–84
Exposures, business, 91

Family limited partnerships, 94
"Fewer, better" activities, 27–41
Financial controls, 87–88
Financial planning, 94
Financial statements, 78–79
Flowchart, 57–59
Focus Day technique, 20–22, 27, 29,
  109–110
"4 Percent Sweet Spot," 15, 17
Fraud, 87
Freedom, 10–11
"Friends and Family" program, 82, 110

Goals:
  building an owner-independent practice,
    3–12, 108–109
  connecting personal and practice, 69–70
  setting annually, 31
GrowMyMedicalPractice.com:
  Action Plan, 36
  asset protection, 92
  complimentary coaching session, 112,
    126–127
  employee termination, 96
  increasing patient volume, 80
  Medical Practice Success Tool Kit, 111,
    121–123
  Sweet Spot Analysis Tool, 34, 35, 60

Time Value Matrix Tool, 16
UBS, 52
Growth strategy, 30–36

Hacker, Bonnie J., 106
High-risk patients, 98
High-risk procedures, 92
High-value work, 15
HIPAA, 52
Hoffman, Jeff, 103
"Home Run" filter, 33–34, 59–60,
  110–111

Inheritances, 94
Insurance, 86, 91, 97
  malpractice, 92, 98
Intellectual property, 52
Internal knowledge, 46

Judgment proofing, 92–94

Kansas Medical Clinic, 43, 45, 46, 71–72,
  74, 75, 82, 104
Knowledge, internal, 46
KPI (key performance indicators), 34, 38

Lawsuits, 89–90, 91
  proactive protections from, 92–95
  reducing likelihood of, 97–98
  what to do if they happen, 95–96
Lead-generation activities, 79
Legal issues, 90–91
Level One practice, 10, 11
Level Three practice. *See* Owner-
  independent practice
Level Two practice, 10, 11, 19
"Leveraged Time," 15, 16, 29, 30
Liabilities, 91
Liens, 93
Likeability, 97, 98
Limiting Factor, 32–33
LLCs, 93, 94
"Low-Hanging Fruit," 33–34, 59–60, 61,
  82, 110–111
Low-value work, 15

"Magic 1 Percent," 15, 17–18
Make Their Day philosophy, 71–72
Malpractice, medical, 90–91, 92, 98
Margin analysis, 27